UNLEASHING
the POWER of
SMALL GROUPS

UNLEASHING
the POWER of
SMALL GROUPS

Essential Group Facillitation Skills

MARK LUTZ

MILL CITY PRESS

Mill City Press, Inc.
2301 Lucien Way #415
Maitland, FL 32751
407.339.4217
www.millcitypublishing.com

Scripture quotations taken from the Holy Bible, New International Version (NIV). Copyright © 1973, 1978, 1984, 2011 by Biblica, Inc.™. Used by permission. All rights reserved.

Printed in the United States of America

ISBN-13: 9781545603406

TABLE OF CONTENTS

INTRODUCTION:

The Power of Well-Run Groups

JESUS HAS THE power to transform lives. The Church as the body of Christ is intended to play a part in that transformation process. Traditionally, churches have relied on Sunday sermons, Sunday School classes, and mid-week Bible studies as tools for growing people. More recently, there has been a shift underway in the Church. Congregations are adding another tool to their repertoire: small groups of various types.

Life Groups, as the name implies, enable people to live life together. The paradox of today is that as technology increases the ways a person can be plugged into the happenings of the world, more people are reporting an increasing sense of isolation and loneliness. Viewing the world through social media lets one stay anonymous and often passive. Life Groups identify a small number of people that a person can know and be known by. Discipleship or Accountability groups are similar to Life Groups with even greater intentionality of urging members forward in personal development. Support and Recovery groups help members address and grow through difficult and painful times of life.

Some churches are even using small groups in place of traditional growth methods. The potential advantage of small groups is this: in addition to needing to know what God says in his word, people need help to know how to apply his truth to their particular life circumstances. They also need support as they attempt the difficult work of bringing their lives into alignment with God's will. The one-way communication of teaching, as happens in classes, is good for informing and instructing. The back and forth communication of small groups allows people the opportunity to wrestle with challenging truths, explore what it will mean if they begin to live by these truths, and get encouragement along the way, if new lessons don't go so smoothly.

To grow spiritually, we seek to understand what the Scriptures mean. We also have to understand what's inside us that makes it difficult to live out what Scripture tells us. Besides divining the mysteries of Scripture, one also has to discern the mysteries within oneself that stand as potential obstacles and barriers to integrating truth into daily living. As Paul says in Romans Chapter 7,

> [15]*I do not understand what I do. For what I want to do I do not do, but what I hate I do.* [16]*For I do not do the good I want to do, but the evil I do not want to do – this I keep on doing. What a wretched man I am! Who will rescue me from this body that is subject to death?*

The two-way communication of small groups is more likely to enable self-exploration and insight than is the one-way communication of a lecture in a class.

Be advised however, not all small groups are created equal. There's no magic that guarantees small groups will definitely be more effective than classes. There are certain characteristics that make small groups powerful. Sometimes a small group has those characteristics, and sometimes it doesn't. There are many instances of small groups going toxic and imploding. When people get real with one another the best and the worst in them comes out. If the facilitator doesn't know how to constrain the worst and encourage the best in people, small groups can create problems. This may be why some church leaders are resistant to small groups. In the early days of adopting small groups at the church I serve in, we found that when we just launched a bunch of groups by gathering people together and picking one to be the leader, some did pretty well, some were kind of flat, and some were dysfunctional and blew up in ugly, hurtful conflicts.

Currently, when people complete one of our support/ recovery groups we encourage them to guard the progress and healing they've gained by continuing to live in community. We steer them toward our life groups. On occasion, I've had the chance to talk with someone after he or she has made the transition from support group to life group. Eager to hear that this person is doing well, I ask for an update. Often I'm disappointed to hear that the person tried a small group, but soon quit going. When I ask why, I hear things such as, "It seemed too surfacy," "It didn't quite feel safe," or "I didn't feel challenged."

The truth is, we ruined them. In our support groups we use the knowledge and skills you're about to learn. They experienced the power and the benefit that these skills bring. They then expect that all small groups enjoy the same depth of experience and growth. While I have to admit that it isn't always the case that a group knows how to create a safe place where people can share deeply and experience the power of God's grace and truth, I hold out hope that it will become reality more and more as we move into the future. The skills you are about to learn will work in all types of small groups: life groups, discipleship, support or recovery groups. The only difference is that with greater vulnerability on the part of the members, greater commitment and discipline is required of the leader to master and use these skills with consistency. But the skills themselves are useful, and I would say essential, in all levels of small groups.

As you read through this material, you may begin to feel apprehensive about how you will remember all of this when you are on the spot to lead a real small group. I expect my students to retain a very small amount of information in our initial training. It is just too much to remember from one hearing. We follow up our class with an apprenticeship. Students are paired up with veteran group leaders. I think it is realistic to expect apprentices to begin to recognize the skills covered in this book as they observe their mentors leading groups.

At the end of each small group meeting, the mentor and apprentice take time to debrief the group experience.

Throughout the course of the apprenticeship, the apprentice is given the chance to observe and then try doing the skills himself. He begins with those skills he believes he can do from previous experience or training. In subsequent group times, the apprentice attempts to do various other skills. The mentor confirms or coaches based on the success of the apprentice. Gradually, the apprentice and mentor work through all the skills one by one. They use a skills checklist that matches the skills taught in this book. Students are likely to begin to learn and gain skills over the several weeks of apprenticeship as they participate in real-life small groups.

My hope is that you will have a similar environment for learning these skills. This type of training program may not yet be available at your church. If you are unable to learn in this preferred environment, there is a website address at the end of this book that directs you to training videos which can be used in a classroom setting, or for independent study. If you can at least find a study partner to learn with, it will increase your chance of success and enjoyment in learning. If you're already leading a group, you can slowly introduce the skills little by little. If your group has been going for a while and good has come from it, you are probably doing some things well, either from training you've had in other places or from natural talent and instincts. You can afford to add skills slowly as you are able. God's grace will cover you and your group, even while your skills are increasing. But in time, you (and hopefully, your group) will begin to notice a positive change in the nature and productivity of your group time together. The fact that you're reading this now gives me hope for healthier, life changing community becoming the norm in our churches.

Chapter 1

WHO CAN BE A GROUP LEADER

WHEN SOMEONE FIRST considers leading a small group, there may be hesitations and self-doubt about whether he's ready to lead a group. Is group leading only for the super spiritual, or can anyone lead a group? The answer is "no" and "no." No, you don't need to be a super spiritual giant to successfully lead a small group. But there are some qualities that matter, that not everyone has. The following is how you'll know if you could lead a small group.

In a nutshell, here are the basic criteria for a small group leader:

1. Proficiency In Facilitation Skills – expressing the relevance & power of God to affect a life
2. Spiritual Maturity – walking with Jesus over time, faithful in adversity, obedient when obedience is not convenient
3. Emotional Wholeness – being a mostly-healed, wounded healer, having more scars than open wounds
4. Relational Connectedness – living in community with the team to do ministry and for personal discipleship

Let's take a longer look at each one.

1. Proficiency in Skills This book (or class) is intended to help you gain proficiency in small group facilitation skills. Aptitude is the ready ability and potential to become competent at a skill. Skills are developed when a person applies study, practice, coaching and more practice to raw talent. Proficiency is aptitude realized; reaching one's full potential. While you do not have to become a master before you can start, a certain degree of mastery of the skills is beneficial. A group leader is always learning, always improving, but there is a minimum level of proficiency that allows a leader to be successful. How do you know when you've reached the minimum level of ability? That's why the number four criterion is important. More about that in a minute.

2. Spiritual Maturity This one is probably one of the more difficult criteria to define. How do you quantify something as ethereal as someone's spiritual condition? Yet, it's worth giving consideration to because it affects one's ability to lead a group well. While there is no unit of measure for spiritual maturity, there are some indicators worth looking for.

Maturity is something that is developed by spending a significant amount of time hearing from and cooperating with Jesus. It's difficult, if not impossible, to manufacture instant maturity. And time in and of itself does not guarantee maturity. But time spent with Jesus usually results in the character of Jesus being developed in the life of the disciple.

One character trait we look for is teachability. We want to know that a person is not just open to, but eagerly seeks out new information and new experiences that will cultivate a deep relationship with Jesus. We ask about time spent reading the Scriptures. We ask about past small group experience for discipleship. As people go through our training, we look to see if people can surrender their current understanding to a new idea that has a Biblical basis and is confirmed in real life experience. As students go through their apprenticeship, we look to see who can receive feedback from their mentor or coach.

Related to teachability is humility. Perhaps the deadliest seduction for a leader is the temptation to think, "Because I'm the leader, I must know everything. I must be able to answer any and all questions my group may throw at me." This thought can either result in pride or paralyzing self-doubt. God is the only true expert. The rest of us are only continual learners. As a leader, sometimes the best thing you can tell your group is, "I don't know," especially if that's the truth.

Imagine yourself leading a group of hurting people, some whose lives are in shambles. A few feel hopeless, desperate and are struggling most of the time. Others are self-confident and smug, thinking they have it pretty much together. Some are expressing great emotional pain; while others seem numb or deny their pain. A number have "hit bottom" in their personal lives; they have serious marriage problems, financial difficulties, job losses, housing needs, or even legal problems. The majority want to obey God, but a few individuals are angry at Him. Some in the group lack good social skills as well.

What do you do? Panic? Play God? Try to fix everybody? Give up? Are you going to feel like a failure if some members of the group don't seem to "get it?" What if they continue to struggle in their personal lives? What does this mean to you? Are you a failure as a group leader?

No, it just means that you are not the one in charge; everything does not depend on you! God speaks and works through all the facets of a group and you are simply His fellow worker. You can do your part and trust Him for the results. A seasoned group leader knows to persevere through difficult times in group leading. And so, as an indicator for who might be a successful group leader, we look for people who already have a track record of being faithful in adversity.

It's not so hard to do what God asks of us when the sun is shining, the wind is at our back and all is going our way. It gets harder when we face opposition. Fear of being judged as narrow-minded, self-righteous, or holier-than-thou can drive us toward fitting into the culture rather than standing out from it. And to be honest, it's not always convenient to do what God has asked. Many people in today's culture find it inconvenient to save sex for marriage, and so, they don't. Many people find it inconvenient to give a tenth of their income to the local church, and so, they don't. Many people find it really inconvenient to deny themselves their material desires in order to give to people who will never be able to repay…and so, they don't. Jesus didn't say we would find it inconvenient to follow Him. He said we would have to take up our cross and die to self to follow him. In those moments when you are trying to do what God has asked of you, and it's so hard that you cry out to God, "You're killing me here!" God says, "I told you I would." This level of surrender, faithfulness in adversity, obedience when it is not convenient, this is the kind of character that makes for good group leaders.

3. Emotional Wholeness A safe and effective group leader is one that recognizes that all he or she will ever be is a wounded healer. The most dangerous leaders are those who perceive themselves as experts who have arrived. The key to successful leadership is the awareness of my own brokenness and my continuing need for Jesus to work in my life. The most compassionate people are those who are in touch with their own woundedness and dependence on the Lord.

> *Praise be to the God and Father of our Lord Jesus Christ, the Father of compassion and the God of all comfort, who comforts us in all our troubles, so that we can comfort those in any trouble with the comfort we ourselves receive from God. Quote from New International Version (NIV)*

In 2 Corinthians, the apostle Paul describes the way God transforms our painful struggles into something constructive. God gives His comfort and compassion to us so that we can comfort others in their times of need. This is the Biblical pattern for becoming a group leader. Group members respond better to a leader who has "been there," someone who understands their problems, knows what to do about them and can truly offer hope.

It is preferable for a leader to be a mostly-healed, wounded healer. This means that while he may have not yet reached total healing and still have work to do, he has more scars than open wounds. Group leading is a full contact sport. A group leader may get jostled around a little relationally as he leads the group. Unfinished work in the leader may be drawn to the surface. Group members may act out of their issues occasionally. If the leader still has very tender places in his heart from the past, these can be triggered by group members as they are in the process of doing their work. If this is a possibility, then perhaps now is the time for the leader to be in a group, rather than leading a group.

4. Relational Connectedness Having a relational connection to a team that has been doing group leading longer than you have is your safety net. Other people are the best source of objective feedback about how you're doing. That's why relational connection and the accountability it provides is so important, not just during the equipping process, but throughout your time of group leading.

Although accountability is a concept that can conjure up fear in the best of us, all leaders should have someone they consider to be a person on whom they can depend for spiritual guidance. Some of us have come to believe that we need to live in fear because of the oppressive relationships we have been placed in under the guise of accountability. This fear can be alleviated, if we remember that accountability is developed out of relationship.

Because all people have a propensity to stray off the straight and narrow at one time or another, having people we can depend on in times of joy and pain can prove helpful. When it comes to spiritual warfare, we learn to cover each other's backs. Accountability is not someone telling you what to do, or how to run your life; nor is it someone acting as a go-between for you and God. It's not someone who is more spiritual than you, teaching you the right way to deal with life circumstances. Accountability exists when a person or group of people develop the trust to allow them to disclose their true personalities and struggles. You find it in other people with whom you can be vulnerable; ones you can turn to at any time for counsel or comfort, and trust they will help you up when you fall down.

Accountability is most helpful when it is self-initiated. It is most threatening when it is initiated by others. If I wait for others to intrude into my life to scrutinize me and tell me where I've messed up, I will fear accountability and probably shy away from it, missing its benefits. If, however, I initiate the process and open my life up voluntarily to another for inspection and feedback, I find that rather than being something that is hurtful, accountability protects me from many potentially hurtful things.

The relational connection we have with our ministry team is a conduit for relational connection with God himself. The reason we are able to take the calculated risk of having group leaders who are imperfect and unfinished and not fear that they will hurt the people who come to our groups is that God is the ultimate source for power and life for the group. Remember what Scripture says,

---

"I planted the seed, Apollos watered it, but God has been making it grow. For we are co-workers in God's service" (Quote from NIV)

Much of the good that comes out of our small group ministry happens in spite of us rather than because of us. Having the humility to embrace this reality is the secret to having peace, hope and longevity in small group leading. There's actually something quite freeing about acknowledging that you're not the final word in someone else's life. Knowing that you're just one part, a very important part, but just one part of God's instruments for changing people's lives is both humbling and liberating.

The weight of responsibility for the people in any group you will lead is shared among these five elements:

1. Group Leader: You form the group, choose the materials, recruit the members and establish the format. You are committed to the group, accountable to church authorities and responsible for seeking outside counsel when you get stuck. You're a shepherd and a role model, not a dictator, caretaker or therapist.

2. Group Rules/guidelines: Rules govern the behavior of the members and provide structure and protection when there is friction in the group. Some rules are negotiable, while others are not. Rules clearly

delineate what behavior is acceptable and what is not. Group rules become a contract in which members make commitments to the group.

3. Group Members: People are the heart and soul of the group. They give care and encouragement to each other and model responsibility for its life and leadership. They function like a second family, a living organism, capable of sustaining itself with minimal direction from the leader. When the group is struggling or stuck, God works through the collective wisdom and experience of its members to suggest solutions.

4. Group Materials: These establish the direction for the group and provide a basis for discussion. They offer the information needed for changing lives, as well as a home base to return to when discussions get off track. Some groups do not use many materials (just a meeting format, brochures, and a few standard readings.) Others require more (perhaps a workbook, leader's guide, the Bible, and homework assignments).

5. God Himself: Jesus has promised that where two or three are gathered in his name He would be there. That's a very reassuring promise for small group leaders. Have the faith and humility to trust Jesus to do what He says.

A group leader is not a super-human, spiritual giant who single-handedly rescues people from their vices and their circumstances. A group leader is a reasonably grounded, mature, whole individual who turns the gifts God has given her into well-honed skills. Along with the community of God's people and other resources available, this person is used by God to accomplish the growth and healing that a particular group of people are ready to receive.

So that's the answer to who can lead a small group; those people who have proficiency in group leading skills, who are spiritually mature, have emotional wholeness and are relationally connected for support and accountability.

Chapter 2

LISTENING: THE SECRET OF MAKING HEART TO HEART CONNECTIONS

IT IS WORTH noting that I am addressing the skill of listening out of sequence. Listening is one of the skills used when facilitating the heart of a group meeting. The first bit of work a leader does is to prepare for the group and open the group meeting. Then the leader facilitates the group experience using various skills of which active listening is one. I talk about active listening now to give the maximum amount of time to practice listening while you learn about the other aspects of group facilitation. Whether you are learning to facilitate groups in a class or individually, I hope you will practice listening throughout the rest of your study.

I use and recommend this strategy because listening is the base upon which all the other skills work. I will go so far as to say that the other skills do not work well without listening to people first. So, if you are not going to apply yourself to the work of listening, save yourself the time; put this book down now and go do something else. Listening is that crucial to the effectiveness of every other skill that is used to facilitate groups. I feel a little like that fictional character from the TV sitcom Parks and Recreation, Ron Swanson. A famous quote of his is,

> *"Bring me all the bacon you have. Wait, I worry that what you just heard was bring me a lot of bacon. What I said was, bring me all the bacon you have. Do you understand?"*

I feel that strongly about active listening when leading small groups. Listening is the single most important skill to learn if you desire to lead safe and effective groups. Listening is what makes all the other skills work. Wait, I fear you heard me say that listening is just one of many skills a group leader might try to pick up. What I said is, Active Listening is the single most important group facilitation skill there is. If you are not practicing active listening regularly in your group, you are facilitating a mediocre to poor group experience. Do you understand? So now, bring me that bacon!

The skill of active or empathic listening is the foundational skill to successfully leading life transforming small groups. It's so important that I expect a good group leader to use this one skill about two-thirds of the time they're leading. The other third of the time is spent using all of the other facilitation skills available. I'll explain first why listening is so important and then how to do it well.

Numerous times in the gospels we read that Jesus knew what was in the hearts of people. He knew what they were thinking.

Jesus knew their thoughts and said to them, "Every kingdom divided against itself will be ruined, and every city or household divided against itself will not stand. If Satan drives out Satan, he is divided against himself. How then can his kingdom stand?" (Matthew 12:25 & 26)

"Why does this fellow talk like that? He's blaspheming! Who can forgive sins but God alone?" Immediately Jesus knew in his spirit that this was what they were thinking in their hearts, and he said to them, "Why are you thinking these things? Which is easier: to say to the paralytic, 'Your sins are forgiven,' or to say, 'Get up, take your mat and walk'? (Mark 2:7-9)

Now while he was in Jerusalem at the Passover Feast, many people saw the miraculous signs he was doing and believed in his name. But Jesus would not entrust himself to them, for he knew all men. He did not need man's testimony about man, for he knew what was in a man. (John 2:23-25)

Knowing what is in a person's heart can be helpful when trying to influence people and be an agent of life transformation. Lacking the divine power and insight Jesus possessed, our best chance to learn what's in the heart of a person is to get her to tell us and then listen really well.

The Science of Active Listening

Many people have had some kind of training in Active or Reflective Listening in their jobs. Basically there are three parts of an active listening response.

1. The content: the facts, the who, what, when, where, how
2. The feeling: the emotional response that person had to the content; mad, sad, glad, scared and confused in matching intensity; low medium or high.
3. A tentative opening: "It sounds like..." "It seems like..." You're not telling a person what she thinks and feels, you're asking the person whether you've heard her correctly. You don't want to be so forceful in your declaration that if you're wrong she'll be too intimidated to correct you. You're also giving her an invitation to look at what she's said in order to gain greater understanding, an invitation that she can accept or decline until she's ready.

Here's an example of how a reflective statement would be constructed. Someone says to you...

"People are always asking me to do things for them, people at work, friends, family. I get overwhelmed sometimes. Some of the stuff seems like things they

> *could do for themselves but just don't want to. But
> I feel so guilty if I ever tell anyone "no" so I end
> up stressed doing their work and they're having a
> great, fun life."*

There are several ways you might respond to this individual… let's look at the different possibilities. You might respond with the phrase:

> *"You shouldn't feel guilty for not helping your
> friends. You should feel guilty for letting people
> walk all over you."*

Or

> *"You don't really feel guilty, now do you? After all,
> God can forgive anything can't He?"*

Even if you are motivated by a desire to shake a person out of a stuck place or to speak truth plainly and forcefully, responses that invalidate the speaker's thoughts and feelings are the least helpful. This kind of contradictory response is likely to leave the speaker feeling her concerns have been dismissed, causing her to close down any self-exploration or further self-disclosure. Another response you might offer is:

> *"People can be so insensitive and selfish. I used to
> have a friend that did that kind of thing to me and
> I finally had to put him in his place."*

This type of hi-jacking response has the intention of siding with the person in her frustration, demonstrating that you relate to the speaker because you've experienced something similar and offer help in the form of an answer: that the speaker should also stand up for herself.

What actually happens within the speaker is that she gets the impression that you are less interested in her and more interested in talking about yourself or correcting her behavior and fixing her problem. She may feel judged as incompetent and weak. She is likely to feel disregarded and unlikely to share further. Another response you might have could be:

> *"That's too bad. I'm sorry people have been so mean to you."*

This is better than the previous two responses but still short of the goal. It is a reaction to what the speaker has said instead of a capturing of what was said. Instead of reflecting what's been said, this response makes commentary about what's been said, "That's too bad." The speaker gets a hint that you are sympathetic to her plight. However, she still lacks confidence that you've fully understood what she is experiencing. She may assume it's because she's just not worthwhile enough for someone to actually track with what she's trying to express. Still another possible response for you might be something like this:

> *"So you're feeling stressed out."*

Or

"So people are taking advantage of you all the time?"

These responses are getting closer. In the first response the speaker has a sense her feelings have been heard, but may not be convinced that you, the listener, understand her circumstances well enough to be helpful. In the second, she gets the sense her story has been heard but she hasn't been persuaded whether you have compassion for her or not. In her thinking you may just as well use your understanding to coerce her into doing something that fits your agenda and not hers. With either, she lacks the complete satisfaction of being fully understood. But this may be enough to keep her trying because it's better listening than she usually experiences. Another response might be,

---

"So it sounds like you're feeling overwhelmed because of all the work you've taken on to do."

Or

"It sounds like you are trapped into taking on more work than you can do because if you say no you'll feel guilty."

Or

> *"It sounds like you're feeling frustrated because you're doing all the work while your friends are having all the fun."*

This is what you're shooting for! Any of these responses demonstrate an understanding of both feeling and content. The speaker is likely to feel understood and continue talking. Notice that each of the reflective statements picks up on different feeling and content. It's not necessary to capture all the feelings and story all of the time. You will frequently make judgment calls about which part of the story is most important to the speaker. You make educated guesses based on the context of what else has been said and nonverbal indicators. This reflective statement serves as an invitation for the speaker's examination, reflection and confirmation. If you guessed wrong about what is most important to her, the person will normally continue because of the confidence she has that she is being listened to. She will likely come back around to it again.

You can go for all the marbles, trying to capture all that was said. That's called a summary statement. The trick is to be very concise, boiling down the speaker's rambling exploration of ideas and feelings to bullet points. Summary statements are most helpful after a speaker has talked for a while and some theme or common thread runs through a couple of related ideas.

Notice that whichever feeling / content item you choose for reflection, the statement is a paraphrase of what the speaker said, neither adding to nor leaving out any relevant bit of that part of the story. These statements are interchangeable with what the speaker said, and are at the same level of disclosure they shared. Still another response could be:

> *"It sounds like you are afraid of saying "no" because it will mean that you're a bad person."*

Or

> *"It sounds like you endure a great deal of abuse from your friends out of fear of being rejected."*

These reflective statements reflect what is unsaid, tapping into underlying thoughts and feelings. Each of these empathic statements reflect more than what the speaker said outright, at a deeper level of disclosure than she chose. If there is considerable trust established this kind of advanced accurate empathy can help people gain insights about things just below their conscious level of thinking and feeling.

However, if it is early in the relationship and trust has not been fully established, this kind of insightful reflection can shut a person down. She realizes you know something about her that she did not yet decide was OK for you to know. This can cause fear about what else you can see about her without her consent. For very intuitive group leaders, one of the biggest challenges is to hold back and just reflect what the speaker said and not what the listener's intuition heard.

The Art of Listening

Some people who are perhaps of a more intuitive person-ality sometimes draw a blank when trying to remember the formula for a reflective statement. We've heard people say, "This is too clinical for me." It's not really clinical, it's just rela-tional. I think what they're reacting to is the technical aspect of "content, plus feeling with a tentative opening." For these folks I explain reflective listening this way. Suppose you're watching a movie that you're really enjoying. As you're watching it, you think, "I'm going to have to tell my friends at work about this movie tomorrow."

Well, at that point you don't start stressing out about needing to remember all the details of who said what to whom, when and where. You don't start taking notes so you can remember everything. You just give yourself to the movie. You let yourself get drawn in. Then the next day you easily remember what you saw. You naturally weed out the subplots that didn't really work. You catch the high points because that's where the human drama was. Human drama is easy to remember. And "human drama" is another way of saying "emotional reactions".

You can do that same thing when listening to someone. When she is telling her story, she's playing her movie on the screen of your mind. Let yourself get drawn into her movie, paying attention to where the drama is. One thing to watch out for is that sometimes her story reminds you of similar experiences you've had. At that point your mind can switch from playing her movie to playing yours. Don't reflect how you felt or how you think you'd feel if you went through something like that. Be sure to reflect what she said about her experiences and what she felt. That's the secret to making a heart to heart connection.

Pushing Through

Even when you understand and are persuaded of the importance of listening, you may find you struggle to do it successfully. You might hear thoughts in your mind telling you that you can't do this. This can be your own discouraged thoughts or it could be input from someone who doesn't want you to get these skills. I've seen the devil at work before, trying to keep people from increasing their abilities. So as a preemptive strike against the discouragement of the devil, let me tell you what he will most likely use to keep you from listening to someone.

What will keep you from listening:
- It feels contrived
- It feels inadequate
- Expression of strong emotions
- Being falsely accused or judged
- Impatience

It feels contrived. To many people who are working hard to do this skill for the first time, it feels contrived, artificial, insincere and formulaic. They fear they will come across as robotic and insincere. They fear they will be perceived as doing something to someone in order to manipulate the other person.

Active Listening is a skill. And like any other skill, unless you're a prodigy, you'll probably start out kind of rough and have to fight your way to mediocrity. With enough practice though, depending on your aptitude, you can reach a level of proficiency or even excellence. This is true for most every skill we've learned. Playing a sport or a musical instrument, riding a bike, all of these things felt unnatural when done the first couple of times.

What is first done with great effort and feeling a bit stilted, can become fluid and second nature. So I don't accept the excuse from our students that, "This isn't natural, I'm just not a listener." I say instead, "You might not be now, but you could be if you'll just practice."

It feels inadequate. In the face of a tragic story or great need, simply listening to someone feels a little like offering, "be warmed and filled." It can seem almost insulting to not do more to alleviate someone's suffering. This feeling comes from underestimating the power of listening and a mistaken idea about what our role as a helper is.

In an instance of a true crisis where someone's coping skills have been completely overwhelmed and she is in imminent physical or psychological harm, it may be that others will have to make some decisions for the person in crisis. But this is short term and even then we are already looking to how we can get the person back to being in charge of her own life.

For everything else short of a crisis, you must learn to trust the process. With more experience will come more confidence that listening first gets your best, but inadequate, human wisdom out of the way, invites the presence and power of God into the situation and begins to empower the person to solve her own problems and live her own life. In time, with experience, you will become convinced that active listening is not only adequate but even essential to helping people grow and heal.

Listening is what lets you join with someone in her struggles so she's not alone. The one thing that makes a bad situation worse is to be alone in it. When prison officials have someone for whom being in prison isn't enough to correct his behavior, they put that person in solitary confinement.

It's a common assumption that if I could just be smart enough, spiritual enough or good enough, I could find the way to trouble free living. The reality is that we sometimes don't have a choice between pain and pain-free. In some circumstances pain is unavoidable. In those times our choice is between pain in isolation or pain in community. We can choose between pain that is wasted pain or pain that is redemptive because it teaches us something or builds strength in us. And there seems to be a correlation between those two. When I experience pain alone, it tends to end up being a fruitless repetition. Often it is only with the help of someone else who is willing to enter into my circumstance that I find the help, perspective and encouragement I need to wring out the value and instruction of painful circumstances. When we listen to people in tragic circumstances we give them the option of not being alone. We can:

- Show love and caring by listening to the stories of people's lives.

- Affirm the worth of the individual.
- Offer hope in Christ.
- Share truth in love.
- Direct people to resources.
- Facilitate an encounter with the living God.

But it all starts with the act of listening. Listening well to the hearts of people is what gains access to their lives and earns the right to hear their stories.

Expression of strong emotions. Live raw emotion can be intimidating, especially depending on your previous experience and comfort with expressed emotion. Deep sorrow or intense anger poured out in your direction can set you back in your chair. Usually the reason is that your compassion drives you to feel like you're supposed to do something to remedy the negative emotional state. The best remedy is for people to have the chance to express and process the emotion they feel. Emotions that are unexpressed accumulate causing other problems. When they are given a voice, they can then dissipate. Their emotions may elicit emotions in you. That's OK. You can survive having an emotion (even us men). This is, to a much lesser degree, similar to how soldiers learn to stay in the battle in the face of live fire. They train for it. You can also. You can learn to listen even in the face of strong emotional expressions.

Being falsely accused or judged. Or even worse, being accurately accused of something. The natural reaction to either is to want to defend oneself. What helps resist this reaction is to remember that people sometimes project issues they have with someone else onto another person who they intuitively sense is a safer person. Often their reaction has less to do with you and more to do with what they're going through. If you can duck and let the accusation go by, then re-engage with active listening, the other person can often figure out the true source of his distress. It can be hard to get the words to come out of your mouth, "So you're really angry at me because you think I'm a jerk." It can seem like you're admitting he is right in his accusation about you, when really all you're doing is acknowledging this is what he believes and how he feels. Often times, the fact that you're listening and not reacting, is the best evidence the other person's judgment against you is false.

If you have done something that was hurtful, you can be big enough to own your mistake and ask forgiveness. Keep in mind that you could have done a bad thing and still be a good person. Listening will still be the most effective way to get through this.

Impatience. After you've led small groups for a while, you'll start to notice some patterns in the dysfunctions people fall into. As the story begins to unfold, you'll recognize a familiar set of ingredients. Your mind will begin to think, "Yeah, yeah, I know where this goes. Let's cut to the chase. I'll tell you how this ends, what to do to fix it and we can be done and move on to happier topics." This may be the umpteenth time you've heard this story but it may be the first time this person has had the guts to tell it. In discipleship work, the journey is as important as the destination. The process a person has to go through is a necessary component for getting the outcome she and you both hope for. This kind of care requires discipline on your part to be patient with and attend to the person while she is doing the work necessary to get where she needs to go. Listening is still the skill that will facilitate that process the quickest.

Now that I've done a preemptive strike on the excuses that are most likely to keep you from listening, let me give you further incentive to master this essential skill. These are the important things that listening does.

Listening affirms the speaker by receiving the gift. Active listening affirms the speaker by receiving the gift of her sharing. Active listening affirms the person and her contribution to the discussion. It is a way to acknowledge and honor the gift that person has brought out of her deep heart and risked sharing with the group.

Imagine if you gave someone the perfect gift. You thought carefully about her interests and likes and picked something you knew she'd enjoy. What if when she opened your gift, she just looked at it, quickly said "thanks" and moved on to open another present. You'd feel disappointed. You'd want some kind of reaction; "Oh I love it", "I needed one of these!" or "I've got just the occasion when I can wear this." Until we see that the gift has been really received well, the act of giving is not complete or completely satisfying.

When people share private treasures from their deep heart, they're looking for something more than "uh-huh" or "thanks for sharing". They want to know that their gift has been fully appreciated and received. That's what reflective listening does.

Listening confirms understanding. Active listening confirms that understanding has taken place for the listener and the speaker. As the listener I may be sure I've accurately understood the speaker. However, the speaker is the ultimate judge and sometimes I'm confronted with the fact that I don't always have such a firm grasp of the facts as I thought I did. When I take the time to paraphrase back to the speaker what I hear him saying, I can get confirmation or correction. If I stay at it until I get confirmation, I can then have greater assurance I accurately understand what's being shared with me. When I hear him say, "Yes! That's it", it confirms for me that I'm tracking with him.

Listening demonstrates understanding. I may be confident that I've understood the speaker, but until the speaker is confident I've understood him, I haven't earned his trust. Demonstrating that I've understood him by reflecting back what he's said is more convincing than saying, "I understand". From his perspective, until I show I have understood him, he is left with three possibilities; I do understand, I might think I understand but I'm wrong, or I don't have a clue what he's said but don't want him to know. In the case of convincing people that you've understood them, the action of reflecting back what you've heard them say definitely speaks louder than the words, "I understand just how you feel."

Listening encourages exploration and understanding. Sometimes we have accurately captured what the person has said, but when he hears it back he realizes it's not what he meant. Often times people get valuable insights from hearing their own thoughts reflected back at them. It's as though they're hearing it from a different perspective. On more than one occasion a group member has responded to a paraphrase of his story with, "I've never thought of it that way before, that's helpful." This is astonishing to the listener since he's only repeated back what he's just heard the group member say. But this truly is helpful to people. Now it is confirmed the person understands himself better.

Listening creates a safe environment, free of hidden agendas. We insist on proficiency in active listening because it promotes a safe environment. People struggling with problems are used to having family members, friends and co-workers telling them what they should do. There can be apprehension on their part when first coming to a small group. They might be wondering, "is this going to be one more place where someone is going to try to impose their well-intentioned but unwanted agenda upon my life"? Active listening shows them we are willing to make their agenda our agenda. We follow along with them, exploring their story at their pace, until we have understood them. Then, input could actually be wanted and welcomed because we've demonstrated restraint and a regard for the individual.

If you attempt to solve a person's problem for her, you are implying that you don't believe she is competent to live her own life. When you facilitate a person's learning and solving of her own problems, you demonstrate confidence in her and in God to work out the issues in her life.

Listening grows interest in, care of and love for others – listening becomes a Spiritual discipline. When I first began studying how to help people, I learned the skill of warmth – showing genuine caring, empathy – the skill of demonstrating accurate understanding and respect–the skill of showing unconditional high regard. I realized that there were many times when I didn't really care. I didn't care enough to try and truly understand another person's world and I didn't always have respect for that person in light of what I was hearing.

At some point it occurred to me that God cares about all people, including this person before me now. God understands him. God maintains great respect for him. I decided that I at least wanted to treat people as God would. In order to not be a hypocrite though, I admitted to myself and to God that this was an act of obedience and the attitude didn't yet fully resonate in my heart. I asked God to change my heart while I attempted to do what was right. And He did! I found the act of treating people warmly, respectfully and in an interested way served as a spiritual discipline that expanded my heart and transformed it to be more like Jesus' heart. The more I listened to people and to God at the same time, the greater my understanding grew about the effects of a sinful world on people and the enduring worth and value that's innate within us by reason of our design. For the sake of my own spiritual condition, I needed to listen to people even more than they needed to be listened to.

Listening provides you with what to say next. One thing that stops folks from coming along side of hurting, struggling people is the fear they just won't know what to say. That's only true if you think you are in charge of solving their problems and making their lives turn out well. But if you believe that is God's responsibility, and your only job is to be a vessel of His power and a facilitator of healing, then you don't have to come up with wise answers to the profound mysteries of their lives. You only have to join with people while God does His work. And if to do that, you choose to be a good listener, they are going to feed you your next lines. Paraphrase back to them what they just told you and you'll find the conversation moves along nicely and they get the support they need.

Those of us wanting to be used by God to help transform people's lives must listen in order to hear and understand the needs of individuals. Human nature's tendency is to listen so we can plan our next brilliant bit of commentary or rebuttal. You have to restrain yourself from that impulse and really tune into what the person is sharing with you. Remember the best way to break a habit, like trying to fix people, is not to try to stop that behavior but to busy oneself with a better behavior. So, get busy listening!

Chapter 3

STARTING GROUP WELL

Choosing Good Resources

PART OF STARTING well is choosing good material for the group to use. Even though you may plan to spend significant time sharing your lives with each other, most groups benefit from having a sense of purpose and progress. Having something meaningful to study and learn from gives the group a sense they're getting valuable input and fresh ideas that will help them grow. Fortunately, there is a wealth of great material out there to choose from, whether you're looking for a Bible study or a study on life issues. Choose from well-known authors or materials with good reviews from trusted sources, and you'll do fine. Running your study selection past your pastor or group supervisor will ensure that what you are presenting to your group has your church's endorsement.

You can write your own studies if you have a gift and a passion to do so. This can be time consuming and challenging to maintain without burnout over a long time. You don't want to dread group night because of intense preparation if it's not necessary. Using professionally produced materials provides the group leader with a predetermined structure to follow. A beginning group leader might find this comforting as she is trying to remember and master all the group facilitation skills learned in her recent training.

DVD series with accompanying leader's guides offer the greatest structure for a group meeting, then books with accompanying workbooks, then books without workbooks. CD's could also be used. We recommend that they be used for short excerpts only. Many people are visual learners and can be distracted without some type of handout or outline to follow along with.

For support and/or recovery groups, we suggest materials produced by well-known authors like Henry Cloud & John Townsend, Gary Smalley or Robert McGee. You may also find one page handouts here and there that you'd like to use as well. These can be a helpful addition to your toolbox.

Activities that act as metaphors for life principles can be powerful ways to facilitate a lesson or a growth step. Some examples are a trust walk, releasing helium balloons with prayers or emotions we're giving to God, burning papers with sins we're asking God to forgive, writing letters to people we need to reconcile with (living or deceased), or artwork, such as making collages from magazine pictures to express emotions about a particular life experience.

Give consideration to age appropriateness and safety of any activities you plan to use. For example, you might do a trust fall from a table top backwards into the arms of peers with teenagers who are nimble, strong, flexible and bouncy, but choose not to do that with senior adults who are less so.

You might need to avoid activities involving touch if there could be people in the group who are survivors of sexual abuse. If you choose to do an activity with some emotional or physical risk, offer an option of participation at a level each person is comfortable with. Someone may be willing to be a spotter, a coach or a cheerleader but decline to do the risky part of the exercise.

What to Do Before You Lead a Group

Here are some things to do as you prepare to lead the group:

- Show up 15–20 min early to prepare the room and welcome group members.
- If you're meeting at a church and have the benefit of using audio video equipment that's provided for you, confirm that the requested equipment is in the room, and that everything is functional. Make sure that you have enough chairs and that they're in the arrangement you want.
- Make any copies of handouts that you'll want to distribute.
- Pray with your co-leaders & apprentice.

Let's look at each of these areas in more detail:

Show up 15–20 min early to prepare room and welcome group members. "Standard Church Time" is when a large majority of people show up, usually 10 – 20 minutes after the advertised start time. If the group leader shows up on "S.C.T.", she is late. If the leader doesn't show up early, she is late.

When a group leader is late the group members may begin to question the leader's commitment to and preparedness for the group. Being at the group early instills confidence in the participants. Being early allows the leader to prepare mentally and spiritually for the group. Being late can result in the leader feeling hurried, harried, distracted and unsettled. Group members can pick up on these feelings and be affected by them. Being early is a proactive investment in the success of your group.

Confirm that the requested equipment is in the room, and that everything is functional. You may want a DVD player, VCR, laptop computer, projector, flip chart, etc. Make sure you have enough chairs and that they are in the arrangement you want. Should you find something you've requested for your group is not in the room, you have time to collect it. If you are meeting at a church, there are often facilities personnel available to help you. Acquaint yourself with the procedures for requesting equipment from the staff. Taking the time to get to know the people who set up the rooms for you can gain you extra cooperation if something you requested is not there. Remember to not take out your anxiety at finding the room different from how you expected on the people there to help you. You want to maintain a good working relationship with your teammates for the future.

Make any copies of handouts you'll want for your group to study or have as a resource. When doing groups at a church you may have to get a copier code from a staff person. Get to know how to work that copier before your group is about to start. Be realistic in your estimates of how many copies you'll need. Most churches work on a tight budget and copier expenses can add up when several group leaders are making copies and they make several copies per evening every evening.

Pray with your co-leaders and/or apprentices. In a Christ-centered small group, it is essential that you seek God to help guide you. In the Old Testament, God told Joshua (another leader stepping into new territory) "Have I not commanded you? Be strong and courageous. Do not be terrified, do not be discouraged, for the Lord your God will be with you wherever you go." (Joshua 1:9 NIV) It can be a little daunting to enter into a group of people and presume to do something that will facilitate growth and healing. You might feel that some of the people coming to your group have more experience and maturity than you have. The anticipation that some people might bring needs greater than you're capable of meeting could cause some apprehension.

To attempt to lead a group in our own power is probably folly. And if you're concerned about what's about to take place, imagine how the people in your group might feel anticipating opening themselves up in authentic vulnerability to other people. But we don't have to do ministry in our own strength. We have at our disposal the all-powerful God of the universe, so I say, let's cheat! Invite God to exert his power to work in and through you to make your small group leading fruitful.

Prayer is that discipline that reminds us we are not sufficient in and of ourselves to accomplish the task before us. We diligently do all we can to train and develop ourselves, choosing to give God our best, all the while knowing it will never be enough. Prayer invites God's presence and power into our groups. Prayer opens up our spiritual hearing so we can respond to God's gentle redirections during group time. Our prayers open up access to God's power for the benefit of the people in our groups.

Here's What a Successful Set-Up Looks Like:

- Group leader and apprentices are present 15 minutes before start time
- Group leader has made any needed copies before group start time
- Group leader has confirmed needed equipment is in room before start time
- Group leader has prayed for the group with co-leaders and apprentices before group

Opening the Group

Greet people with a smile. A genuine smile puts people at ease. This is especially true when people are coming to a group for the first time. They may feel a bit apprehensive, asking themselves, "What kind of people are going to be in this group? Will they like and accept me? Will they ask me to say or do things I'm not ready for?" A smile communicates that this group is a warm welcoming place.

Sometimes the group leader may be a bit apprehensive about the group starting themselves. "What kind of people will come to my group? Will they accept me as their leader? Will they view me as competent?" This apprehension could make it difficult to smile genuinely and naturally. A little mental preparation can help. A natural smile can be developed by rehearsing some positive self-talk. Self-talk refers to the conversation always going on in our heads. Here are some examples.

> *"Some person may very well get free of some kind of burden, bondage or baggage during our group. "*
> *"God may want to do for someone in my group, what He's done for me."*
> *"Each person is dearly loved by God and He brought them to my group for care and attention."*

This kind of self-talk helps us build a sense of expectation that God is likely to do something significant for the people and use us to do it. That's something to smile about.

Another skill that will help break the ice and allow you and the arriving group members to smile is small talk. While you are waiting for the rest of the group to show up make the effort to chat up those who are there. Silence contributes to nervousness and coldness. Small talk puts people at ease and contributes to warmth in the group.

To even mention this as a thing to do seems ridiculously obvious to some. There are people who find that small talk comes naturally to them. "They've never met a stranger" the expression goes. There are, however, other people who find the task of talking to strangers with no identified topic or discussion question difficult, even painful. The greatest challenge is when the group is new and there hasn't been enough interaction yet to know people well. If you are one of the latter, you are probably an introvert. Welcome to the club and know that you too can be a good group leader. We just have to plan differently than our extroverted cohorts. Having a few stock discussion questions in mind helps. Here are some examples of small talk discussion starter questions.

"Did you have any trouble finding us tonight?"

"How was traffic?"

Talk about the weather: *"Was the – rain, snow, sleet–coming down hard when you were driving in?*

"Was work busy today?"

"How did you hear about our group?"

"Have you been attending this church long?"

Notice that the questions don't lead to anything deep or require much thought or risk of self-disclosure. They just prime the pump. They are the excuse for people to be talking. When there is light friendly talking people are usually put at ease. Often there will be someone in the group who chats readily and they can keep the ball rolling with just a little prompting. Soon others will join in. If the conversation winds down, you simply go to one of your next questions or ask a question to one of the other members who hasn't talked yet. What you are likely to find is that when you are talking with people you will find it easier to smile at them. And when you are smiling you will see that smiles are contagious.

Announce and invite. As people gather they are likely to mingle and chat. Left alone people will likely do this as long as they are permitted to do so. It might feel rude to interrupt the conversations going on around the room to start the group. Yet this is precisely what you must do if the group is to start on time and have the full amount of time allotted to accomplish the goals of the group.

Announce that it is time to begin and invite people to join you: "It is now 7:30 and time for our group to begin. If you will take a seat, we can get started." If this is said loudly, clearly, confidently but warmly, most people will join in. You can give people a few seconds to finish a conversation in which they're in mid-sentence and then begin.

If someone is oblivious to the invitation because they are lost in their conversation, some gentle, positive peer pressure can be brought to bear. Using "we" in the invitation "we can get started" implies that "we" are being held up by the ongoing conversation. If the group leader will remain quiet, watching the conversation with a smile on their face, others in the group are likely to look in that direction as well. The absence of background noise, combined with peripheral vision picking up people's attention being focused on them, will normally break the spell of a riveting conversation.

Maintaining a smile and using an affirming, warm tone of voice to announce, "Great! Let's begin" will establish your leading without coming across as overbearing.

Another challenge to starting group is when few people are present at the advertised start time. The temptation is to wait until enough people have arrived to begin. The group leader who sticks to his plan to announce and invite within five to seven minutes of the advertised start time begins to train the group to arrive on time. The alternative is for late comers to train the group that it will start five minutes later... then five minutes later... and so on and so on. When late comers arrive, acknowledge their arrival with a smile and a nod while continuing with what you are saying. If someone interrupts with an explanation for why they are late, announce what is going on and invite them to join while maintaining the momentum of the group. It could look something like this:

> Late arriver: (interrupting conversation) *"Sorry I'm late, traffic was awful and my boss gave me a project right at 4:30 that's due tomorrow."*
> Group leader: (smiling): *"We are reviewing last week's work. Please, come on in, take a seat and join us."*

By saying "we are...reviewing last week's work... going over guidelines... meeting new guests" rather than "we were just..." shows that there is an activity in progress. "We were just ...going over the guidelines, etc." sounds like "what we were doing wasn't all that important so it's no problem to have it interrupted."

We want to gently influence behavior toward the group's goals without being patronizing, parental or insulting. We do this by giving feedback to people about how their behavior is affecting the group without embarrassing them in front of the group. We'll look at how to give feedback in greater detail in a later chapter.

Open with prayer (optional). While you most certainly will be in prayer for your group prior to its starting, you have an option to include prayer as part of the beginning of your group or not. If you are leading a Bible study or Life group, most people attending would not be caught off guard if you opened the group with a prayer. If you are leading a Support or Recovery Group not everyone in attendance is necessarily as comfortable being included in prayer. For some people, a support or recovery group might be their first contact with church and they are coming not so much with a desire to find God, but to find help with their problems and relief of their pain. In their minds they are taking a risk that they will be able to tolerate the "religious stuff" while getting the help they seek.

In an attempt to be sensitive to a seeker who is trying to find out if they fit in with this group of people, a leader may elect to start slowly and work up to spiritual activities and language. Choosing to wait to include prayer until the close of group or later in the group's development could allow the seekers in your group time to get to know people and determine that this is a safe place before introducing them to things they are unfamiliar with.

If you have some doubt about every member's comfort level with spiritual matters, you can wait, let one of the group members raise the topic and watch each person's reaction to the discussion. When heads nod in the affirmative, when people join in the discussion, when people listen attentively with a relaxed expression on their face and an open body posture, you have indicators those people are comfortable with and open to a discussion of spiritual things.

When people are absent from the interaction, when heads are down, eyes looking at the floor or around the room, when people have a puzzled or anxious look on their face, when their arms and/or legs are crossed, these may be indicators that these people are uncomfortable with the discussion of spiritual things at this time and are withdrawing from the group interaction.

If you determine that the people in your group will either appreciate prayer at the beginning of group or be able to roll with it, you could offer a prayer along these lines. Keep it simple, mostly an invitation to God to come and work in your group and inviting assistance for the group to be open to what God is going to do. The prayer need not be elaborate or eloquent. A prayer as simple as this would be enough, "Jesus we invite you to come to our group and do what You would do, Amen." Avoid slipping sermonettes or teachings into the prayer. Do whatever teaching you plan on doing, directly, as part of the group discussion.

Use prayer time as an opportunity to express the Father's heart for His children, expressing praise for His attributes such as mercy, compassion, love, forgiving, healing, truthful, mentoring etc... This kind of prayer will likely be less threatening to a newcomer. Keep in mind that this prayer is to help the group begin and it does that by helping people begin to know what they can expect to experience in the group time ahead.

After you have led prayer for a couple of weeks, you might want to invite someone from the group to open in prayer. Your prayers will serve as modeling and give an example of what the opening prayer is to accomplish. This gives participants a sense of ownership for the spiritual component of their group.

State the purpose of the group. When people begin a new small group experience there can be feelings of apprehension and nervousness. What helps alleviate some of this anxiety is making the unknown known. We help people make a decision about what their comfort level will be in our group when we explain two things, what they can expect from the group and what the group will be expecting from them.

When the group leader gives a concise description of the intended objectives of the group and a summary of how the objectives will be accomplished, this paints a picture for the participants. That picture replaces their anticipated fears and "what if's". This helps group members to shift from preparing themselves for the worst case scenario to anticipating positive experiences.

A group leader will want to express the purpose of the group each time the group is open to new members. In the case of a closed group, this is usually the first three weeks before the group closes to additional people. In an open group, which is open to new members every time the group meets, the leader would do this anytime a new person shows up. If we want every person in the group to cooperate with the group agenda, then every person needs to know what the agenda is. The only way they'll know that is if we clearly communicate it to them.

Here is an example of how a group leader could explain what the objectives of the group are and how the objectives will be accomplished for an open, ongoing support group.

"In this group we will address a wide range of topics. You can work on something small that is a minor irritation you just can't seem to get past or a major life disrupting adversity. What we will do is provide a place where people can get things off their chest. Sometimes it's helpful to just talk out loud about what's troubling us and have someone listen. Often we can figure things out ourselves given this opportunity."

"We can also ask for feedback from the group if we would like. Sometimes other people have been through similar things and we can learn from them what did or didn't work well for them. At the very least, we will make sure that no one has to go through their adversity alone. When we listen to

> *one another and care about each other, we find the*
> *strength we need to keep pressing into our partic-*
> *ular issues."*

Since this group is ongoing, the description addresses the process more than the content or specific outcomes. Here is an example of what it might look like to describe the purpose of a closed small group.

> *"In our group "Hunger for Healing" we will be*
> *using the video series from Dr. Keith Miller to*
> *examine the 12 steps of recovery. While the 12*
> *steps are widely used in work with alcoholism we*
> *will consider how the 12 steps can be helpful in a*
> *wider range of life controlling issues."*
>
> *"We will take one step a night. The video will give*
> *us an introduction to what the step means and how*
> *people have used it. After the video we will have*
> *discussions about how we might make application*
> *of the step in our own circumstances."*
>
> *"When we are finished with group we will have a*
> *basic grasp of the 12 steps and will begin to put*
> *them to work in our lives to get freedom from life*
> *controlling patterns."*

Since this group follows a curriculum to a conclusion, more can be said about expected outcomes. Note that both purpose statements are relatively concise, ten sentences or less. It is not necessary to go into great detail. This gives people enough information to start to form a picture of what lies ahead. You don't have to answer every possible question. A little mystery can lead to curiosity and interest that keeps people coming back. We do however want to give enough information to reduce anxiety about the unknown.

Review the Group Guidelines. The purpose statement informs people about what they can expect from the group. The group guidelines help people know what the group expects from them. When people are not sure what the parameters of group conduct are, they may have the fear that they are going to accidentally do something wrong and embarrass themselves. By clearly stating group guidelines up front, everyone can have confidence that they can participate without being surprised by any unspoken rules.

The rules of a group are designed to benefit and protect individual members, the group experience and the leaders. Good guidelines create a safe atmosphere in which individual growth and healing can occur. They do this in several ways:

- Rules offer protection
- Rules provide structure
- Rules set standards for group behavior
- Rules teach new ways of relating to others

Some group leaders may feel as though they are being parental giving adults rules to follow. This doesn't have to be the case. Whether a leader comes across as parental will be determined by how the guidelines are presented. We are not insulting adults with restrictive constraints. We are giving rules of play for a unique interaction. Group guidelines are the guardrails that keep us safely on course while engaging in an adventure that requires some risk taking. Guidelines show that thought has been given to the risks involved and these are the precautions taken for the sake of risk management.

People not only find reassurance from knowing what's expected of them, they also find comfort in knowing this is what the other group members are promising to do for them as well. This is why I always conclude the reading of the guidelines with asking for clarification of understanding and a commitment to follow the guidelines. I first ask if there are any questions about the guidelines; if any of the guidelines are stated in such a way as to cause confusion.

After answering any questions about the guidelines, I get confirmation from the group that they understand the guidelines. "Does everyone understand the guidelines I've read?" I look around the room making eye contact with each person. This elicits a confirmation from each person. As I look around the room, most people will follow my gaze and they also register acknowledgement of understanding from each of their group mates.

I then ask if they can agree to abide by these guidelines for the sake of the group. I ask everyone to respond in a way that I can recognize, either verbally or nodding their heads in the affirmative. Again, I look around the group at every person to acknowledge their answer. When I'm doing this the group members again are following my gaze around the room and can see their fellow members answering. I ask everyone to make a commitment to follow the group guidelines to the best of their ability and in conclusion, I give my commitment to the guidelines as well.

It is important to define rules thoroughly right from the start. Beginning this way sets the stage for learning new behaviors while at the same time preventing potential problems. Rules are not intended to be used as "clubs" to keep people in line. But when difficulties start to arise, we are able to refer members back to the guidelines they agreed to follow for the benefit of their group mates. This keeps a corrective action from degenerating to a conflictual battle of wills between the group leader and the members. We simply remind the members of the agreement they made in reference to the guidelines.

As the leader of a small group, you will find that rules help in dealing with problems common to groups. Instead of using your "authority" to confront behavior that hinders the group, any member can refer back to the rule that was agreed upon. Of course, rules will be broken. So-called "problem members" are simply people practicing old survival skills which worked to some degree in their families of origin. They need to recognize when these adaptive strategies are no longer in their best interest and they need to learn new ways of relating to others. Groups are a safe place to experiment. As time passes and the group feels familiar and safe, you may find you are able to let the members take care of guideline violations themselves, rather than coming to their rescue as "the leader".

It is the group guidelines that allow us to offer two groups at once. The first group is whatever the title of your group is, whether it's a Bible study, book study or a discipleship group. The second group is a "healthy relationship skills" group. That's what the group guidelines are: the behaviors that happen in a healthy relationship. Depending upon a person's family of origin, he may not have had an opportunity to learn all of them. The practice of and enforcement of group guidelines may be some folks first chance to practice healthy relationship skills. If they practice them in your group, their ability to do them in their other relationships increases dramatically.

What guidelines to have and how many to have can be different from group to group. A general rule of thumb is the fewer guidelines the better. We want to provide safety while not stressing people out about trying to remember a bunch of rules. The more sensitive the material you'll be covering, the more fragile people will be when coming to your group, the more guidelines the group will need. A group on Sexual Abuse recovery will need more guidelines than a group on Boundaries. A group that will be mostly information transference will need less structure than one that will require people to explore past painful experiences.

Here are some guidelines that are useful for just about any group to follow.

Confidentiality: What is said in the group stays in the group. Obviously, if a person wants to share their own story outside of the group, they are free to do so. Also, any life lessons or principles that a person has learned and is excited about, they can share outside of group. What does not go outside of the group are other people's stories or even the fact that they are in attendance at the group. We keep other people's private matters private.

Limits to Confidentiality: Should a group member disclose that they are having thoughts of hurting themselves or someone else, that they are planning to commit a felony or that they suspect a minor child, a special needs person or an elderly person 65 years old or older is being neglected or abused, we will have to bring into the situation other people for the purpose of preserving life.

In most states there is a legal requirement called "duty to warn". Counselors and educators are typically held to this standard legally. Even an average citizen may be held to account in the aftermath of a tragedy for not taking action to preserve life.

What beginning group leaders hear is that we must break confidentiality if these circumstances occur. This is not always true. What we can first try to do before we rush to break confidence and lose whatever trust we've established, is to invite, encourage and empower the person themselves to make the call. If they are willing to call or are willing to have us call on their behalf, then we are fulfilling our responsibilities without breaking confidence or trust.

If after our best efforts to help the group member make the call, they are unwilling or unable, then we are required, willing and able to call whoever needs to be included. It is important to tell people up front that this is the case for the group so they can give informed consent when disclosing their personal stories. Reminding a group member that this is the policy of your group when making the call may help in maintaining a collaborative effort even if the member was initially resistant to including outside assistance.

For instances of suicidal thoughts, we may need to call family members who are supportive, a counselor the person is working with, a hospital for their admittance or 911. For homicidal ideation, we may need to call the person the ideation is directed towards, family members, friends or counselor or law enforcement. This would also be true for the intent to commit a felony. For abuse or neglect issues we would contact the human services agency for the elderly and special needs person or child protective services for minors in the county the abuse is suspected to have occurred in.

In all these cases we work as a team. Should you be faced with one of these circumstances you will want to contact your coach or the over-seeing pastor of your group for consultation and support.

Self-focus: Most of the stories people will share in a group involve other people, so it is expected that in the telling of their stories we'll hear about those other people. However, it is easy for a group member to slip into a discourse on all the things that other people have done or are doing that are making his life miserable. But if we want any chance at having life change, the focus needs to be on oneself. The group has no power to change people who aren't in the group. In reality, the only person I have any chance of changing is myself. I am the one that I have the greatest influence over; I am the one that I am ultimately responsible for. So we encourage the use of "I" statements and direct group members to focus on their own growth. We ask each member to take responsibility for his or her own feelings and to speak up if something in the group is causing discomfort.

We do not analyze, diagnose or fix other people in the group: We let each person take ownership of their problems, seek their own solutions and take responsibility for what he thinks, feels or does. We do not offer unsolicited advice, tell people what they "should", "ought", or "must" do. We can offer feedback if it is wanted and the best way to know if it's wanted is to ask. Then we use "I" statements owning our experiences, opinions and ideas, allowing the other person to decide if what we're offering is helpful. This includes Scriptures and Biblical truths.

Limit sharing so all may participate: We work to avoid having a few people monopolize the conversation. Everyone, even the quiet and timid, are to have equal access to the time in the group.

Regular attendance: For closed groups, regular attendance is essential for building mutual trust among all the members of the group. Irregular attendance brings into question the level of commitment that member has to the group.

Other rules that might be used for more vulnerable groups could be:

- Prerequisite experience in other identified groups or classes.

- Pre-registration and or interviews to determine readiness.
- No graphic details about slips or relapse experiences that could act as triggers causing another member to fall.
- No crosstalk, only one conversation at a time, when one person is speaking the rest are listening.
- Stay on the subject, we avoid rabbit trail discussions that distract from or delay the work at hand.
- We avoid debates about controversial subjects.
- We refrain from inappropriate humor that distracts from deep heart sharing, or is at the expense of someone else, present in the group or not.
- No dating other members of the group for the duration of the group.

The last skill used for opening the group time is:

Review last week's work and set goals for this meeting. When a group leader can give a concise review of the previous week's work, two things are accomplished.

First, the review reminds and re-emphasizes the important lessons that were previously learned. By assisting group members to exercise their memories of what happened a week ago we are reinforcing and establishing those lessons in their minds.

Secondly, the group leader sets the context for this week's work. By establishing continuity between the weeks we make each individual week's work more memorable. Instead of trying to remember several disjointed lessons over many weeks, group members are remembering a series of lessons through which runs a common thread. When reviewing, you don't need to re-teach the previous week's material, you simply want to state the main learning objectives in their most distilled form. The review can be as simple as reciting the outline you created when preparing for the previous week.

If the leader can show how the work of the last group meeting prepares us for this week's topic, the learning is made easier and retention is increased. Prepare a transition statement that shows the relationship between last group meeting's work and this week's.

Here is an example of what a review might look like:

"At our last group meeting we discussed:

- *How forgiveness is a choice not a feeling.*
- *We learned that it is a decision to release someone from our indebtedness, sometimes in spite of lingering feelings of pain or sadness.*
- *We also learned that the decision is a process, a series of choices made over time, from day to day, sometimes from minute to minute."*

(Transition statement) *"This week we will look at some of the things that can potentially keep us from making the decision to forgive."*

The review is very "cut-to-the-chase", very bottom line. The review should closely resemble the identified learning objectives set for the previous week, assuming that the group successfully discovered those objectives.

Simply hit the main points and then transition to this week's goals. The goals can also be brief but sufficient to set the direction for the evening and begin to focus people's thinking on the topic at hand. The goals could also be a transition into the teaching. As long as the statement of the evening's goals is clear then the participants will be clear in their expectation and mental preparation for what is about to unfold.

Here's What a Successful Opening Looks Like:

- Group leader is calm and expectant, greeting arriving members with a smile.
- Group leader announces that it is time for the group to begin and invites members to join in within 7 minutes of the advertised start time.
- Group leader acknowledges late comers, inviting them to join in the activity in progress.
- Group leader decides whether an opening prayer will be done. Group leader either leads a prayer or asks a member to lead a prayer inviting God's direction and help with the activities ahead.
- Group leader explains the purpose of the group in ten sentences or less, addressing both content and group process, in a way that is easily understood.
- Group leader presents the group guidelines and seeks confirmation of an understanding of and commitment to follow the guidelines from each member of

the group. The leader does this for the first 3 weeks or when any new person comes to group.

- Group leader reviews the main learning points of the previous week and transitions to the goals of the current evening.

Chapter 4

GROUP FACILITATION–ASKING GOOD QUESTIONS

THE KEY TO asking good questions is to listen lots first. It may be tempting to think that in order to help someone grow you need information about them and in order to get information you need to ask questions. That seems logical. But asking someone lots of questions, especially early in the interaction, often results in that person feeling like he's on the receiving end of an interrogation, causing him to clam up rather than speak up.

It is amazing how much you can learn about a person by just listening. But then, there are times when a well-timed, well-crafted question is very useful. It helps to know what the intended purpose is for asking the question in mind. Seldom will you use a question to get information in the course of facilitating a group. More likely, you will use a question to bring clarity to an issue a group member is working on or to get someone started on a path of self-discovery, especially if the person seems to be stuck.

Sometimes someone is stuck in a growth and/or healing issue because of unidentified dynamics at work in his life which are having effects that may be undesirable or even unhealthy. Most often this is due to a lack of self-awareness related to some issue or issues from their past history or in their current functioning. We can assist people in exploring their issues, then finding and gaining insights about such hidden forces with the use of well-crafted questions. Once a person has gained new insight, new possibilities open up for him regarding intentional decisions he can make to initiate change towards an improved future.

To this end, when we hear a group member talk about and around vague, abstract, or ambiguous concepts or events, we assist the group member by helping to make those ethereal entities take concrete shape. Then the person can take hold of them, turn them around, examine them, draw conclusions about them and do something about them. In fact, the skill of asking questions to bring about this kind of clarity is sometimes called the skill of concreteness.

Someone may say, "My life is going badly. I need to do better." What does "badly" mean to him? Has he thought about what specifically is going badly or is there only a generalized sense of discontent? What does "better" mean to him? Does he have any specific expectations of what "better" will look like? How will he know that he has made his life "better" enough?

There are two types of questions we use to help facilitate concreteness. They are:
1. Probing questions
2. Clarifying questions

1. Probing questions. Probing questions get the conversation going. Probing questions are useful to invite people to explore a particular aspect of their lives. Knowing how to form good probing questions will help you get the people in your group to do most of the talking and therefore most of the work, which is our goal.

In general, when someone asks to talk with me about something that's troubling them, I start with a wide open probing question as simple as: "So what would you like to talk about?" Or in a group setting I might ask: "What thoughts has our study prompted in you tonight?"

These questions seem so obvious but it's good to have them in mind. They help you transition from the small talk that's typical at the start of group to the work the group is ultimately here to do. They also give the person permission to go ahead and dive in. It's not uncommon that even though someone asks to speak with you, he may have some hesitancy about actually disclosing what's on his mind. Questions like these give him the little nudge he may need.

After people have told me their circumstances, I usually then ask them something like:

"Out of all that you've talked about what would you like help with?"

Or

"What were you hoping the group could possibly do to help?"

As you've been listening to the story presented, you've probably identified a couple of things that could be addressed, or that you think need to be addressed. You've done some problem analysis and even started to think of some ideas for improving the situation. But on more than one occasion I've been surprised by what it is a person was actually seeking help for. Even if the thing he wants to work on seems like it's not the most critical part of the problem, I still start there because that's the thing he has motivation to work on. And I want to demonstrate to the person that I'm willing to enter his life on his terms and at his invitation. At a later point, after we've spoken to his concerns, I may offer something like...

> *"When you were first talking, I had another idea about something that may also help you with this issue. Would you like to hear what I was thinking?"*

It's difficult to help where you haven't been invited in. But curiosity alone will almost always get you a tentative, "OK, let's hear it."

Once you have an agreement on what it is you'll be working on, the natural tendency is to begin giving all the great ideas you have for a solution. But I usually use a question like this:

> *"You've obviously been thinking about this some. What ideas have you come up with so far to address this?"*

Or

"What have you tried so far and how has it worked?"
(as opposed to "have you tried...")

Questions like these serve two purposes. First they keep the person in the driver's seat of his life. Folks may come with the hope that you, because you're the group leader, will have some brilliant solution that will rescue them. The problem is that a person can simultaneously wish to be rescued and resist any semblance of being controlled. Any quick answer that you give so early in the dialogue can feel like you are putting an obligation on him to do a certain thing he hasn't yet decided he wants to do. Having people share their ideas first lays the foundation that you're interested in a partnership with them and that their part is vital. Questions like these encourage a person to explore what he has already successfully discovered that could be part of the solution. They also reveal if the person already has an emotional investment in a particular solution.

The second value of using questions like these is that they serve as a reminder to me that I'm not in charge of this person's life and I'm not responsible for solving his problem. It's a sort of spiritual discipline that keeps me in the appropriate role of helper and not savior. The people in our group already have one of those and Jesus is much more qualified than I am.

Probing questions invite exploration and offer direction, all the while acknowledging the right and responsibility of the person to make the decisions that will govern his life.

Probing questions direct the group conversation and help it to be productive. Even when you are using professionally produced small group materials, you may realize that not all of the discussion questions the author provided are suited to your objectives, or you just can't see yourself managing the direction those questions will take the discussion. Knowing how to make good probing questions will help you select what of the published material you will use and what you will want to create yourself.

To use probing questions to set up an evening's group discussion, begin with the learning objectives for this session. Then determine what probing questions will lead group members to discover these learning objectives. This is a little reverse engineering. You start where you wish to end up and work backwards. Probing questions serve as the stepping stones that lead people to the desired destination. One probing question leads to an insight. That insight becomes the platform from which the next probing question makes sense. That probing question yields an insight and on and on until you reach your final destination of the learning objective you had in mind.

The strategy is to start with lower risk questions and gradually work towards more challenging questions that may feel riskier. Start general, outside of oneself. Observation questions are a low risk way of getting conversation started: "What have you noticed about...?" "What have you noticed happens when people overextend themselves?" "What have you noticed happens when people bottle up emotions inside themselves?" "What have you noticed about people who are grateful people?"

As people begin to get comfortable speaking in the group you can move to more specific and more personal questions. "When was a time when you wrestled with something God prompted you to do?" "What are you most grateful for in your life?" End with questions that engage group members at an emotional level. "What's going on inside you when God doesn't answer your prayers the way you wanted him to?" Start with questions that bring clarity to the past, then those that yield understanding of the present, ending with those that help construct a plan for the future.

Here is an example: Following the session on anger, questions may develop this way:

"What happens when people bottle up anger inside them?"

"What happens when people let their anger explode?"

"What are some things in day to day life that irritate you?"

These are general questions that engage people at an intellectual level and engage past recollections. Discussion starts outside of the members and progresses toward self-reflection.

"Have you ever been the receiver of someone's anger outburst?"

"If so what was that experience like for you?"

This question moves members toward a more personal experience. This may put them in touch with feelings in the here and now.

> *"Describe a time when you felt very angry. How did you manage the anger? "*
> *"How well did that work for you?"*

This invites the members to evaluate their coping skills and assess any need for growth. It puts them in touch with the successfulness of their current life strategy and may generate motivation and willingness to make a change.

> *"How would you like to handle your anger in the future?"*
> *"How would you like to feel after you've dealt with your anger?"*
> *"Have you seen or heard of ideas you'd like to try in the future?*

These questions build for the future, and lead group members to take responsibility for finding solutions to their issues. For that reason, people can find future planning questions riskier. They are about to declare that they are not a victim of their circumstances, but are responsible for doing something about them. When they openly declare a solution, there comes the accountability of the group later asking how that plan is going. If the individual isn't actively doing his part of the solution, it will now come to light. Even though this may be the path towards growth, healing and freedom, it can still be intimidating. People may need to gradually warm up to the idea of a solution.

1. Clarification questions. Clarification questions help a person move from generalities to specifics. As discussion takes off with the prompting of well-crafted probing questions, you may hear some of the vague talk we first described, "My life is going badly. I need to do better." Clarification questions will be helpful to bring concreteness at these times. Here are some guidelines for creating effective clarification questions.

It is important to know why you want to ask a question: Is it for your benefit, to get more details that you think you need so you can fix him? If so, feel free to not ask that question. These questions frequently distract the person from the train of thought he was on, distracting him from the work he was doing, delaying the insight he was getting the courage to have. If you ask the question for his benefit, because it will facilitate his discovery of an insight, then you are likely to ask a useful clarifying question.

Here are some questions to avoid:

"Why?"

People tend to hear this question as asking for justification, like "Why would you do that!?", so it tends to trigger defensiveness. You can ask the same kind of things using other words that tend not to act as triggers. Such as "What brought you to the decision to do that?" or "How did you come to that conclusion?"

"Don't you think...?"

What this question is really proposing is: "I'm about to give you the right answer. Are you smart enough to agree with me?" You can probably see how this might not promote an open exploration of issues.

Closed ended questions

Avoid asking questions such as, "Do you...?" "Is this...?" "Have you ever tried...". They tend to elicit one word answers and are a clue that I'm probably falling back into fishing for content I think I need to fix or trying to slip in an answer to solve the problem.

Here are some examples of questions that promote consideration and discussion:

"What does (some vague term*) mean to you?"

---

*examples, fill in the blank above:
it, more, better, happiness, successful, good, bad, healthy

"What does that look like to you?"
"How does that affect you?"
"What about that makes you feel...?"

> *"How do you know this to be true?"*
> *"What tells you this is the case?"*
> *"What helps?"*
> *"How do you manage that problem?"*
> *"How does that work for you?"*

Can you see how these questions encourage people to get specific about things they've been thinking about in nonspecific terms? Can you see how these questions would encourage exploration of thoughts and feelings and allow people to gain their insights under their own power? This is what we're aiming for.

After talking with someone for a while and it seems like we're coming to a close, either because our time is up or it feels like we've pretty well covered the issue, I'll often end with a question like this:

> *"We've talked about quite a few things. What of this seems like it might be most helpful to you?"*

Or

> *"Of all the ideas we've talked about, which one do you think you'll be able to try?"*

Followed up with...

> *"When do you think you'll be able to do that, within a week, two?"*

Inviting people to select a course of action elicits their commitment to a solution while leaving them in charge of their life. The trick then is to be sure to ask about the progress in subsequent weeks. For my discipleship group I've taken to writing notes about action steps members have identified for themselves. People appreciate the caring expressed when you ask later about things that are important to them. Just asking about progress creates an accountability measure that improves the likelihood of follow through.

Can you see how we've taken someone from "I've got to do something to fix this problem," to "I'm going to do this specific action, by this time"? We've helped him utilize the principles of good goal setting to come up with something specific, that is measurable, has a time element, and is doable, all of which he's chosen. When that person chooses an action step he will have more investment in completing it because it was his choice, much more so than if he feels like the group leader gave him an idea that he's still not sure about. Even when you give people great advice, great advice still requires effort to implement. If people are not bought into the idea, they can sabotage the plan with half-hearted effort and then blame the group leader for giving them advice that didn't work. Good clarifying questions lead people to discover what it is they are willing to do towards addressing the issue that's troubling them.

After listening lots first (remember, about 2/3rds of the time) there are times when it is helpful for a group leader to give a response that speaks into what the person sharing has said. This is where it gets tricky because it's easy to slip into problem solving and trying to fix the person. The secret is in knowing what to say that offers influence without attempting to control the other person, either her feelings, her beliefs or her choices.

Chapter 5

GROUP FACILITATION –GIVING FEEDBACK

WE ALL HAVE blind spots regarding ourselves. There are things we do for which we lack self-awareness. It may be a behavior we learned so long ago that we do it without thinking, without noticing it doesn't work or has terrible consequences. We may know that we do a particular thing but lack awareness about the impact our action has on others when we do it. This can be just as true for our strengths as our weaknesses. We may underestimate the positive effect we have on people. In selling ourselves short we miss some of the encouragement we need to continue in doing well. Paul says in Galatians:

> 9Let us not become weary in doing good, for at the proper time we will reap a harvest if we do not give up. (Galatians 6:9, NIV)

Getting feedback from others who have our best interests in mind can help us to carry out this Scriptural admonition. So we will look at how to give feedback in four ways:

validating, active wondering, constructive critique and genuine compliments.

Validating. As you listen to people you will often hear ideas, perceptions or choices you don't agree with. You may be persuaded that what you are hearing is inaccurate, incomplete, immature, inconsistent with what God has said and will possibly end up in pain or damage. In order to show respect to people, refrain from judging them or even evaluating what they're saying, until you have listened to them thoroughly. In fact, it makes some beginning group leaders nervous. If I spend so much time listening to people and suspending judgment, will that be understood as me condoning something that I actually believe is morally, ethically, Scripturally wrong or dangerously dysfunctional.

So with this in mind, let me run the risk of making you really uncomfortable by suggesting that another valuable skill for working with people is the skill of validating. Now obviously you can't validate a person's decision to do something contrary to God's wishes or likely to cause damage to herself or others. Though this is sometimes what people ask, even demand of you. Some people insist that unless you agree with their views you are against them. The truth is that sometimes you are for someone and you are against their beliefs and choices that threaten to cause them harm. You may have a different opinion about someone's viewpoint, even if that person is heavily invested in his course of action. So what exactly can you validate and why is it so important?

Even if you can't in clear conscience validate someone's beliefs or choices, you can often validate some aspect of their emotional state that's driving their ideas and decisions. For example, someone may say to you, "No one cares about me. Everyone I've known has betrayed me, even God. I've decided I can't trust anyone and I'm going to cut myself off from everyone."

You are suspicious about such all-inclusive declarations. Is it really true that no one cares about her? If you find yourself caring about that person, then you know for sure that statement is not true. You are pretty confident God has not betrayed her. He may have failed to meet her expectations, but it's not in God's nature to betray someone. Scripture says God's "ways are just and true", Revelation 15:3 (NIV), so you can't authentically validate those conclusions. But you could genuinely offer this, "I think if my life had gone as painfully as yours has, I might be tempted to feel the same way."

The power that comes from validating someone at an emotional level, at a human level, is that it builds an alliance with the person. That alliance is built on an understanding of and empathy for her pain, even if we differ on the reasons for the pain or the solutions for resolving the pain.

Without an alliance it's nearly impossible to influence someone away from distorted thinking or a flawed coping strategy. Without an alliance you are simply perceived as yet another person who doesn't understand her or really care about her. Many people feel alone in their struggles, believing that no one has ever messed up as badly as they have, no one has ever been as stuck as they are, and no one could possibly understand or care about their predicament. If you establish an alliance of empathy you can be seen as someone who is fighting for them, instead of another person who's fighting with them.

So once you've shown yourself as caring and being for them, how do you turn the corner toward trying to influence them towards what is true and life giving? That's where this next skill comes into play.

Active Wondering. When people in your group express ideas that sound irrational, emotionally driven, flat out wrong or even potentially dangerous, a natural reaction is to attempt to straighten such a person out by giving her a good dose of reality. However, the most natural reaction to receiving a dose of reality is to entrench oneself even deeper in the preferred irrational belief and then argue with and dismiss the input that's being offered.

An alternative strategy to direct confrontation is to offer some active wondering. This works fairly well especially if done after some careful active listening and validating. Active wondering is a slightly less threatening way of challenging an idea. Rather than asserting their idea is wrong or foolish, active wondering casts a slight doubt about the original idea and gently proposes a possible alternative thought.

Examples:

Instead of:

"Don't be silly, of course your parents care about you."

You could try:

"It sounds like you're feeling like your parents don't care about you because they're not getting on board with your plan for your future. I wonder if it's possible that they do care about you but they're thinking about some different priorities for your future than what you're currently interested in. What do you think? Could that be a possibility?"

Active wondering tests a person's willingness to entertain a new perspective by inviting her to consider other possibilities. The reality is that until someone is willing to move from her current perceptions and decisions she's probably not going to change. Your best strategy is to do those things most likely to help her become willing. Sometimes, even after you've listened well, validated her emotions and wondered about her current strategies, the person seems intent on following through on her present plan. But watch for subtle cues that her confidence is a little more tentative. Often times a person may leave group saying she's proceeding as she planned. Then by next group time you get a report about how she thought about what you and the group said to her and she changed her mind. Even after you've done your best work as a group leader, the Holy Spirit has to do his job of convicting and convincing.

Constructive Critique. The natural tendency when we're bugged by something someone is doing is to make a broad generalization about them and then give instructions on what they ought to be doing. "You can be so self-centered. You need to be more thoughtful of those around you!" The natural response to critique, even that is given in the kindest of ways, is embarrassment, guilt or shame. The natural reaction is to defend ourselves with excuses, rationalizations or comparisons with others who are much worse than we are. However, we can offer our critique in a way that might nudge the reaction away from shame and down to mere embarrassment. If everything we've done demonstrates real caring and love, then the person receiving the critique just might be able to push through the awkward feelings that come with being busted, receive the feedback and incorporate it to make worthwhile changes.

Here's a template to guide you when giving a constructive critique. When offering this kind of feedback:

1. Share your observations of the person's behaviors,
2. Share your interpretations of her actions.
3. Share how you felt.
4. Invite input.
5. Make a request for behavior change.

1. Share your observations of the person's behaviors. Be as specific as possible. If you can, reference a recent example giving time and place. That will help the person know what you're speaking about. "Last Thursday, when we were at church, you made a joke about my weight in front of our friends."

2. Share your interpretations of her actions. You can share what you thought her intents and motivations were only if you own this as your assumption. "I took that to mean that you didn't care about my feelings or how others might think of me." This is different from telling her what her motives were, "I know you wanted to humiliate me in front of those people!" I can't really know what's in the heart of another person. But I can share what I thought she meant by her actions. In owning this as my interpretation I leave room I might not be right, and I'm letting her know the impression her actions left me with.

I have a friend who takes it a step further. He would say, "I heard you make a joke about me in front of those people and this is what I made up about that...". I used that phrase, "... and this is what I made up about that..."in a disagreement with my wife instead of saying "...and my interpretation of your actions was...". I felt the increased commitment to the notion that it was possible I might be wrong. It felt more vulnerable and I was afraid I was going to lose the argument. But in actuality, I increased the chance I could win my wife's heart.

3. Share how you felt. Using "I" statements here is very important. If you say, "You made me so sad" or "you hurt my feelings", you give the impression you are putting the whole weight of responsibility on the other person. If you say, "When you did that I felt hurt", then you take ownership of your feelings. You leave room that you could have been over-sensitive or mistaken in some way. But again, you are letting that person know the resulting emotions you had when she did what she did.

4. Invite input. "I was wondering if you meant to do that or were aware that's what was happening with me." It is common that when a person has been hurt and is attempting to make this known to the person who hurt them, to make broad generalizations and dictate corrective measures. "You are so insensitive! You have to promise that you will never do anything like that again!" But this doesn't really invite a partnership. This naturally occurring reflexive response doesn't show respect to the person as an adult. It treats her like a child and she will usually feel scolded like a child. It's very one directional.

Instead, the act of offering an invitation to share her point of view encourages a two-way dialogue. This allows for the possibility that perhaps things aren't exactly as I perceived them. But even if they are, the other person has the opportunity to step up and take ownership for what she's done, like a responsible adult, and so she feels like one. And of course, you need to actively listen to what they share. That may be what allows her to get an insight into what drives her behavior.

5. Make a request for behavior change. "In the future, I'd like to ask you to not make jokes at my expense. It hurts and I feel distant from you." You get a better response when you make a request rather than a demand. Most reasonable people will say yes to a reasonable request. But even reasonable people don't like to be pushed around. And in a manner that is perhaps uncharacteristic of them, they may become defiant just to assert their right to self-determination in the face of what they perceive is coercion. The great thing about making a request for behavior change is this, even if the person lacks the emotional strength to fully own up to what they did on the spot, they could possibly still agree to what you ask. Later, when she's had time to process what happened, she may even get her nerve up to come and take full responsibility for her actions.

The examples I've given here reflect an interpersonal conflict. The formula still works if you are acting in a leader role. Suppose one of the members of the group you're leading gets upset because things aren't going his way and loses his temper. He yells and makes unfair characterizations of the church and the other members of the group, then storms out of the room. If you were to seek him out later and give feedback, what might that look like? If we follow our formula, you could say something like this:

"I wanted to talk with you about the other night at group. When you got angry you raised your voice, made some broad accusations about the church and said some hurtful things to your group-mates."

"I thought that perhaps you believed only your ideas had merit and you were attempting to punish us for not agreeing with you."

"I felt hurt at the thought you didn't regard us as valuable members of your team and sad for the rest of the group members for having to experience that."

"I was wondering what really was going on in your mind and heart to cause you to react that way." (Actively Listen)

"I wanted to ask you if the next time you get angry, could you stay engaged with the group, tell us you're angry without yelling and perhaps give us specific reasons for your anger without attacking people's reputations?"

One thing that can make this even more powerful is if what you're giving feedback about is a pattern you've observed before. If so, share that insight when you're sharing your observations. If the other occurrences were recent enough he might remember them, you can give time and place to help his memory. If the instances happened long ago, he may not remember. Keep in mind these are things in his blind spot. Others were well aware of what he did and remember, but he probably does not. It may still be worth mentioning, "I think I've seen this happen with you before." The things that hide in our blind spots hide from our conscious awareness, but our subconscious may still recognize that this is true.

One more element of feedback you can give is when describing what you've observed and the reactions you had, you can float the possibility "I wonder if what happened that night happens at other times and causes you difficulty in other parts of your life, in other relationships?" This is an invitation to see and know something about himself he may be running from. If you have done a good job of demonstrating care and respect up to this point, he just might accept our invitation to stop running and face what's there.

Genuine compliments. Some people coming to our groups might be a little worn out from straining against their growth issue. It can be exhausting feeling strong emotions for an extended time. Some people may be struggling trying to maintain hope in a battle that is dragging on and on. We may need to offer them some fuel so they can keep going. Part of our job is to offer encouragement and one powerful way to do that is with compliments.

Here are some things that will make compliments powerful. The first is timing. If a person has just shared a difficult time she is experiencing or expressed uncomfortable or even painful feelings and you offer a compliment right away, it may seem like you are minimizing her difficulties. Here's how that would look.

Group member:
"I lost my job today and I'm afraid of how I'm going to pay my bills."
Leader:
"You're a smart person with good people skills, I'm sure there is some company out there that would be glad to hire you."

Using a compliment right then fails to acknowledge the fear she just expressed and almost implies she has no reason to be afraid. A more appropriate response would be to reflect:

"It sounds like you're very concerned about how
you'll meet your financial responsibilities."

Then continue to listen as long as emotion seems to be flowing out of the person. You can begin to feel when a person has talked themselves out. There's a silence that's different from the silence when people are thinking. It's a silence that's accompanied with a kind of sigh that says, "I'm done" and then she looks at you like she's ready for you to say something. Sometime after that is a good time to offer a compliment.

The purpose of the compliment is not necessarily to make the person feel better. She may need to feel those uncomfortable feelings for a while as part of her process of healing. The purpose of the compliment is to give encouragement and emotional energy to the person so they can continue.

In addition to timing, a powerful compliment is genuine, character related and behaviorally specific. False flattery is easily detected and usually leaves a person feeling patronized and not valued. Therefore, complements must be reflective of actual traits. For the purpose of offering encouragement in the process of growth and healing work, compliments about specific behaviors rather than physical attributes have more strength. For example: "You look nice today" has some value. A stronger compliment would be:

"You've shown great determination, by getting
yourself out of the house and here to group, feeling
as bad as you have been."

Here are some other examples of possible growth and healing compliments using the criteria of genuine, character related and behaviorally specific:

> *"I can see it took a lot of courage for you to share such personal things with the group tonight."*
>
> *"You showed a lot of dedication to God by choosing to forgive the person who hurt you so much."*
>
> *"I appreciate the diligence you show by always being at our group on time and being prepared."*
>
> *"I feel valued when you speak the hard truth in a loving way to us in the group."*
>
> *"I admire your perseverance in not giving up during a trial that has lasted as long as this one has."*

By recognizing a character trait, you affirm her personhood. By including a specific behavior, you reinforce that constructive behavior and demonstrate you have thought about what you've said, you mean it and you have the evidence to back it up.

A general compliment of "You're such a nice person," or "You're so kind," may be general enough that a person could dismiss it as just our attempt to be nice or that we are insincere. Remember the people who need encouragement the most are the people who think they deserve it the least. They can be hard to convince that this compliment is true of them. Making the compliment specific helps them to grab onto it.

The same principles that make genuine compliments powerful for individuals work in groups too. Offer compliments in proper timing, after the feelings have been expressed and acknowledged. Offer compliments on character traits with specific details. It may be that you offer a compliment to an individual shortly after she's shared, specifically for her. You may wait, identify a theme of positive actions members are doing and offer a group compliment. An example of a group compliment might look something like this:

> *"I am so impressed with how you all have shown caring for each other tonight by receiving each other's stories with attentiveness and grace."*
>
> *"I want to thank those of you who showed courage in sharing your stories with us tonight and thanks to those of you who showed great respect in how you received the gift of those stories."*

Chapter 6

FACILITATION–SELF-DISCLOSURE

THERE IS A place for telling your story. The important part of self-disclosure is knowing why, when and how to tell your story. Many beginning group leaders believe they need to share their story to show the group they truly understand. Active listening works better to demonstrate convincingly that you understand what the person is saying. Novice leaders sometimes believe the more of their story they tell, the more connection they are making with their group. Actually, the longer the leader talks about his own story, the more the group wonders if the leader is there for them or just needed an audience to talk about himself. They may actually begin distancing from a leader they perceive as being self-absorbed.

Here are some great reasons for telling your story:

- Modeling vulnerability – breaking the ice, getting things started.
- Normalizing their experience "You're not the only one who's been through this."
- Reduce the fear of judgment. I'll show you my flaws first.

The time for telling your story is usually towards the beginning of a time of sharing to get the group going or whenever the group seems to be stuck. Telling your story helps if the group is stuck because of fear about being judged or uncertainty about the assignment or question. You're going first shows them how to proceed.

How we tell our story is very important. It is helpful to have some details. Sharing a vague story is almost like telling no story at all. Share enough details to be truly revealing and vulnerable. Offering up the emotional aspects of your story, not just the facts, invites the group into your world and into your heart. That is when people feel a connection.

Your story must be concise. Taking a long time to tell your story disrupts the flow of the work of the group and shifts the focus from them to you. You want your story to be short enough it sparks ideas for them about how to tell their story and then quickly gives them the opportunity to talk before they lose their nerve or forget what they had to say. You don't want the group lost in your story. You want to facilitate each person getting in touch with their own story.

Usually to tell your story well you need to do some preparation. You may want to write out your story. In your first draft you can include all the gory details. This is often cathartic for leaders. Getting out the whole story now can help you reduce the back-pressure to empty your emotional tank. After you have written thoroughly about your story, you can then edit it. Looking at your story in black and white before you share it helps you to see the peripheral points you can take out and the main points to focus on. You might even practice telling your story. You can try talking in front of a mirror, into a voice recorder or practicing on a friend. Time yourself to have an accurate idea of how long you will have the spotlight on you. Sometimes we think we haven't talked for very long when actually we have.

In review, a good self-disclosure shares enough detail and emotion to be truly vulnerable and is concise enough to get the group sharing again while barely missing a beat.

Chapter 7

FACILITATION–REDIRECTING

THERE CAN BE times in the course of a group when things are beginning to get off track. Sometime, someone will break one of the guidelines, probably in innocence or possibly in indifference. Perhaps someone is monopolizing the time, or someone is talking in circles drifting further and further off track. Maybe someone begins to play Jr. Therapist trying to fix one of the other group members.

Sometimes the first intuitive clue it's happening is when you start thinking to yourself, "Someone should really do something about this". It's likely that if you're thinking this, then others in your group are probably thinking it too. The difference is, you're the group leader, so that "someone" is you! The way to keep the group moving in a productive direction is by using the skill of redirecting.

Some mental preparation is needed to get you ready to redirect behavior. One feeling many beginning group leaders have when confronted with the need to redirect is fear. There can be a fear of being perceived as bossy or controlling. We imagine that if we redirect someone's behavior, she and possibly others in the group who are watching the interaction will think, "Well who are you to tell me what I can and can't do?"

First off, though we might fear it, most people won't be thinking that. Secondly, if anyone is thinking, "Who are you to tell us what we can and can't do?" the answer is, "You are the group leader." As the group leader you have been commissioned with the responsibility for maintaining the safety and productivity of the group. You have authority given to you from the overseeing pastor and from the church, to intervene at any point intervention is needed.

If it helps, you can tell yourself, "Not only am I allowed to redirect inappropriate behavior, I'm required to." The group leader is like the lifeguard at the community pool. It's the life guard's job to blow the whistle if someone is about to dive into the shallow end or is running on slippery wet concrete. If a group member does something that could be hurtful to themselves, to other individuals in the group, or to the group as a whole, it falls to you the group leader to intervene and prevent harm. So be assured, it's OK for you to redirect.

You may feel a fear of being rude. From the time we are very young, most of us are taught that it is rude to interrupt while someone is talking. Then one night, in your group, someone is talking and talking and talking. The more he talks the less his conversation has to do with the group topic for the evening. You're waiting for him to take a breath so you can jump in and redirect but he won't. Somehow he's learned the ancient Mayan technique of breathing through his eyelids so he can talk without pause.

You have a dilemma. Either you interrupt the person to redirect him, which feels disrespectful based on your upbringing or you allow him to go on and on which is disrespectful to the other members of the group. Remember, they came with the understanding they too would get a chance to participate and the group would stay on the subject as promised. What do you do?

What you do is begin to retrain your mind. While it is true that normally it is impolite to interrupt someone who is talking, there are times, and this is one of them, when it is actually the most respectful thing to do. Redirecting inappropriate behavior respects the group who came with an understanding the group would be safe, productive and would be about the topic advertised. To let one person take the whole group off track is a disservice to the rest of the group.

There is also a kindness shown to the person who is being redirected. Have you ever been in a circle of friends where one person has... something green in his teeth... toilet paper trailing from his shoe... his zipper down? When he finally discovers it for himself, that person is outraged, demanding of the friends around him, "Why didn't one of you guys tell me? You let me go around embarrassing myself."

We all hope that our friends are good enough to stop us from embarrassing ourselves by persisting in some unflattering behavior of which we are unaware. We want to be good enough friends to the people in the group that we would redirect them from adverse behaviors of which they are oblivious.

You may feel frustration or anger when someone breaks a group guideline. The thought going through your head at this time might be, "They're not doing it right and they're messing up my group." With this thinking there can be an impulse to punish and correct rather than redirect. A competition can form, in the mind of the group leader, about who's in charge of the group. This can result in an adversarial feeling towards the offending group member.

The solution is to learn not to take breaches of the group guidelines personally. In most cases people aren't intentionally trying to ruin the group. And if they did break a guideline on purpose, there usually isn't any malice involved. And even if there was malice and intentionality, that's somewhat to be expected. People who need the community found in groups, whether they are support/recovery groups or general discipleship groups, usually need them because of some relational deficit, some dysfunctional pattern, some brokenness of heart, spirit or character, some expression of sin working itself out in their lives. We shouldn't shame them or fault them for being where they are. That's just the nature of our work and of the people we've chosen to serve. How will people get to a better place unless someone has sufficient compassion on their situation, tolerance of their baggage and a willingness to educate them in small group behavior and etiquette? It's amazing how much easier it is to redirect when you are calm inside. It's easier to be calm inside when you remind yourself, "This testing of the guidelines is to be expected."

When you've done the necessary mental preparation, you are ready to redirect. It is best to do the redirection at the time of the infraction. In a calm, confident tone of voice announce, "I'm going to jump in here." If the person talking is doing so without taking a break to breathe, you can start by using their name. "Hey Bob, I'm going to jump in here." For most people there is no sweeter sound than that of hearing their own name. Most times that will stop someone in their tracks and give you their full attention. Many times the whole group will look at you in stunned disbelief. They too were raised to never interrupt. The pause created by their shock gives you enough time to wrestle control of the group out of the hands of the person breaking a guideline. Then you explain why you are jumping in. Stating things with the best possible spin allows a way for the guideline breaker to save face. After explaining how we are deviating from our guidelines, I offer what we can do that would be consistent with the guidelines.

Here are some examples:

One of the group members begins advice giving, telling another member what they should do.

"I'm going to jump in here. It seems like we're beginning to drift towards advice giving that we said we wouldn't do." (I remind the group we all agreed to follow the guidelines.) "It sounds like you have something you think would be very helpful to John." (This is the best possible spin, affirming a likely positive motivation.) In order to avoid giving advice, we can do a couple of things. We can ask John if he's ready for input. If he is, we can offer our ideas using "I statements" and allow John the final decision about whether this is what he needs to do next. Would you like to try that?

A group member is going on and on about how the other people in their life need to get their acts together.

"I want to jump in here. Remember we said we wanted to keep a self-focus in our group. How could you apply the things we've been discussing to your life?"

Or

"As you'll remember at the beginning of group we mentioned how it's impossible to fix people who aren't here. Can you tell us more about you?"

Most people won't be too offended with this kind of redirection. In fact, it's a bit of a compliment to be invited to talk more about oneself.

Immediately after someone has shared deep emotion, a fellow group member in an attempt to cheer him up offers a cliché response.

"I'm going to jump in here. It sounds like you care about the pain Sally is in and want her to feel better. I want to make sure we don't accidentally minimize the experience Sally is telling us about (offers a best possible spin of being unintentional). Sometimes if we are too quick to console without demonstrating we've heard the hard stuff, it can feel like we're saying it's not really that big a deal or we don't

> *want to hear about painful things. I'm sure that's*
> *not what you mean to say. So I'd like to make sure*
> *we've captured what Sally is trying to tell us."*

Then do a reflective statement that acknowledges Sally's pain. This models what appropriate behavior would look like.

It can sometimes feel like these breaches of the guidelines are unnecessary interruptions that are keeping us from the important objectives for the evening. In actuality, these interactions can be valuable lessons teaching people life skills they've not yet had the opportunity to learn in any other environment.

Dealing with Members Who Persist in Violating Group Guidelines

A group leader may choose to let a small infraction of the guidelines go by if it caused no harm to the group. To correct every and all guideline infractions could itself be disruptive to the small group process. The group leader must address those violations that are more blatant and more likely to cause some harm to members or to the process.

Then there are those times when someone just isn't getting it. This will require a more direct and firmer intervention. It is best to do this outside of the group time because we want to avoid embarrassing the person in front of the group. At the end of group, warmly ask the person if you can talk to them for a moment. You may want to step outside of your group room away from other people to provide some privacy.

It is best to be direct and to the point. This kind of feedback, like compliments, is best if it's specific and is an objective description of behavior. For instance, telling someone, "You're talking too much" may be less helpful than if you said,

> *"You probably aren't aware of this, in the past three weeks I've noticed that you've taken fifteen minutes or more in sharing your ideas and that you offer thoughts several times in an evening when there are others who haven't yet shared. In each of those instances, I've attempted to redirect the conversation to let others participate equally. I have two concerns. First is that as I continue to interrupt you, it could begin to feel like a personal attack. I have nothing against you. I'm not angry with you. But I will be redirecting anyone that is breaking the group guidelines. My second concern is for the other members of the group. I'm concerned about whether each person who has come will get a chance to do the work he or she needs to do. I know some people are more timid and take a while getting up their nerve to speak. I want them to have a chance to participate too. I'm wondering what thoughts you might have about how we can correct this."*

We begin by assuming the best, "You probably aren't aware of this." This communicates that we're not out to make this person a bad guy. Then we offer our observations, describing behavior. We are careful to avoid interpreting motives or attaching labels. We just describe the behavior in specific measurable terms. "… in the past three weeks I noticed that you've taken 15 minutes or more in sharing your ideas and that you offer thoughts several times in an evening when there are others who haven't yet shared."

I offer my concerns, expressing concern for that person as well as for the group. I'm also making a commitment to correct this behavior as long as he persists in it. I then invite the person to share the problem with me and share in constructing a solution.

We hope the intervention results in the person gaining insight about their behavior and offering to do better. In this case we affirm the person, "I appreciate your willingness to hear this feedback and your willingness to work on this. That shows humility and character."

If things don't go as well, if the person doesn't seem agreeable to align his conduct with the group guidelines, our job is a little tougher. We restate the guidelines and reinforce that abiding by them is a requirement for continued involvement in the group. It may help to review how failure to comply with the guideline negatively affects the group…

"It is very important that we not try to fix other members of the group. Each person is responsible for his or her own life. When we fail to honor that, we communicate that he is not smart enough, not capable enough to live his own life. That's just not what this church believes. We believe each person with God's help can determine his or her own life.

> *If you wish to continue in our group, you will need*
> *to abide by these guidelines. I hope you will be able*
> *to stay with us."*

This allows the person to make the decision about whether he stays or not. We are not throwing him out of group. We are clarifying the decision before him; conform his behavior to the guidelines like everyone else is doing or stop participating in group. Then he decides whether he will continue. Staying in the group and blatantly ignoring the guidelines is not one of the choices.

There may be times when a group leader will need to redirect a behavior not specifically covered by the group guidelines, either during group or in individual conversations with group members outside of official group time. Jesus would sometimes redirect people from behavior that was detrimental. In the Gospel of John chapter five we read of a conversation Jesus had with a man he had healed.

> *[13]The man who was healed had no idea who it was, for Jesus had slipped away into the crowd that was there. [14]Later Jesus found him at the temple and said to him, "See, you are well again. Stop sinning or something worse may happen to you." [15]The man went away and told the Jews that it was Jesus who had made him well. (NIV)*

Jesus began by meeting the person where he was and serving him as he had need. But eventually Jesus did get around to addressing the root nature of his circumstance. As we work with people, we may see they are stuck in behaviors that aren't helping them. The most merciful thing we can do is to redirect them lovingly. So after we have joined them in their pain by listening to their hearts, we will want to speak to root causes of the trials they're going through.

Paul says in Galatians 6:1:

> [1]*Brothers, if someone is caught in a sin, you who are spiritual should restore him gently. But watch yourself, or you also may be tempted. (NIV)*

The skill of redirecting will help us to do just that. You will occasionally hear people describe patterns of behavior that are obviously (at least to you) contributing to their distress, yet they seem committed to continue. One of our standard ways of leading people to identify unhelpful behavior is to ask the question, "How's that working for you?"

You see, it's not enough that we recognize the behavior as ineffective. People are only likely to change a behavior when they assess that it's not working. It is the act of acknowledging that very fact that begins to rally their commitment to do something different. Sometimes you'll notice that people are slow to admit the failure of their current strategies. That's because all behavior is purposeful. There is a reason why we do what we do. There's a payoff that we perceive benefits us in some way from the action we're taking. The hesitancy to give up a behavior is linked to the desire to not lose the payoff.

Sometimes the benefit is well understood, but other times it's felt instinctively at a subconscious level. So to help a person assess what he is doing, we might ask point blank, "What does this behavior do for you, what does it get you?" This may be the first time he's thought about the behavior in such an intentional and direct way.

Next, we may have to lead them to evaluate the cost. That's usually even farther from their thinking. When the people in our group begin to see both the cost and the benefit associated with their chosen behaviors, we can invite them to weigh the two against each other. People are motivated by pain reduction more than they are to growth and self-improvement. Human nature is such that we will gravitate to short-term relief and immediate gratification, oblivious to the long-term costs.

You may have to reflect the benefit and cost back to them, "It seems like you're getting some immediate relief, but your solution creates more grief for you in the long run." Then we can invite them to consider a better alternative, "Would you be interested in a solution that addresses your immediate concerns but has less long term negative effects?" Everyone knows the right answer to that question, "Yes, of course I would!" Even if they still feel ambivalent about giving up their familiar coping strategy, there's a pressure to agree with the obvious rationality of the question. People will usually at least entertain a new idea. They may have to warm up to it over time, but even this is progress.

Delaying gratification and enduring legitimate suffering for a greater good are skills that must be learned. That's part of growing up. We may have to teach and nurture people into a more mature way of living. As they try new behaviors and experience superior results, they become more persuaded of the value of this way of living. Many people have never considered doing a cost/benefit analysis on their choices. But we have learned that people seldom change until the pain of staying the same exceeds the pain involved with change.

Suppose you have someone in your group whose focus is on what other people have done to make her life miserable. She is in no way acknowledging or speaking about her part in the problem or the solution. Then in a gentle tone you could say something like this:

"Joan, I'm going to jump in here for a minute. It seems like we're spending a lot of time talking about other people. I just don't have any idea how you and I can straighten them out from here. I hear your frustration about what they're doing and I'd like to see you get some relief. I wonder if a strategy that might work better is if we focus on things you can do to reduce the impact of their actions on you. Tell me a little about how you've felt and what you've considered doing to take care of yourself in this difficult situation."

I start by using her name because it's effective at stopping a conversation under momentum. There's no sound sweeter to the ear of a person than the sound of his or her own name. It will usually stop her in her tracks. Then I declare I'm taking charge. In a gentle, kind but confident tone of voice, I declare that I am leading. The surprise of being interrupted also aids in getting her to stop. The tone of your voice reassures you mean her no harm. That's also curious to some people. Now you have her attention!

Then I point out the behavior that I want to redirect and I explain why I'm doing what I'm doing. I'll often use myself as the fall guy, "I don't know how to fix that person", "I'm not smart enough to solve this for you", "My responsibility to all the people of our group limits the amount of time I can give to this." This is a great time to assume a one down position. I admit certain limits and weakness I have in order to keep myself out of expectations to do more than I can do or to do what's not going to be effective.

It also helps if you can explain how the behavior is not going to benefit them. Joan isn't going to get the change she seeks by us talking about how bad the other guy did her dirty. Adults respond well to explanations. "Because I said so" only works with children and even then it doesn't work well in the long run. There's a good reason for your redirection. Explain it and gain her cooperation.

Then, I speak to the heart. I want to affirm that while I'm no longer willing to go in the direction we were heading, I'm still for her. And when I tell someone "no" to something, I like to tell her what I can say "yes" to. "No, we won't spend our time talking about other people. Yes, you can talk about yourself." Now how can anyone get mad about that? You've just given permission to take the spotlight and receive all the attention. It's hard to complain about that.

People may feel awkward about being redirected. If they are shame-based people to begin with, they will be tempted to feel guilty. I just ignore all of that by keeping a warm, kind, interested demeanor. I don't get mad; I don't act like they've committed a foul. I act like it's completely natural and still part of my sincere concern for them, which it is. And so most people, while being a little dazed and confused about what just happened, will roll with it.

Let's try another one. You're talking with someone who's going on and on about minutia, obviously avoiding the real issue he needs to talk about. Some people feel safer in the details of factual content rather than entering the emotional realm of interpersonal conflicts. So you might say something like this:

"Bill, I'm going to jump in here because I have a limited amount of time for group and the time is getting by us. I want to make sure you get a chance to ask for whatever help you hoped the group could give. Could you jump to the part where you want help with something?"

There are times when a redirection is not an invitation but an outright refusal to participate.

"I need to stop you right there because I think we're starting to move into gossip and I won't participate in that. If you want to come back to talking about you, I'd be glad to continue, otherwise we're done here."

Or

"I understand you are very angry about your situation and with me because I won't do what you want me to. It's OK for you to be mad at me, but I don't accept people yelling at me and calling me derogatory names. If you'd like to apologize and speak in a civil tone, I'd be glad to continue. Otherwise we are done."

These are obviously more extreme situations and they happen less frequently. What helps in redirecting, even in these tough exchanges, is to stay emotionally calm. I have to do a lot of self-talk to pull that off. I tell myself things like:

- Their behavior reflects more about them than it does me.
- They're not a bad person; they're just stuck in a bad behavior.
- I'm not a bad person because they're mad at me.
- I'm not a bad person because I couldn't meet their expectations.
- Even this redirection and their resulting frustration could be a necessary catalyst to their future growth.

Can you see how redirection like this is firm but gentle? Redirection shows respect for the individual while also showing mercy by calling him out of harmful behaviors and into that which is life-giving. New group leaders have expressed concern about knowing how firm to be with a redirection. They would never want to hurt someone by speaking too harshly with them. (These group leaders are generally nicer people than I am.) We use a metaphor to help guide us. It goes like this.

Some people are like butterflies, gentle and delicate. All that is required to redirect them is a feather. A gentle word spoken plainly with warm fuzzy affirmations attached will clue that person in and motivate them to adjust their actions accordingly. Redirection accomplished! Some people, however, are not butterflies.

Some people are like goats. They are a little more committed to their current behavior. When a goat decides to lay down and not budge, there is more mass and substance to get moving than with a butterfly. This may require a different tool than a feather. What is needed is something more substantial, like a bamboo rod. A more direct word spoken with greater conviction and less warm fuzzies will be required. There's no need to be disrespectful to the person. You are only being more firm about the request for behavior change. If you swat a goat with a bamboo rod, you can usually get him to go where he needs to go. Some people are not butterflies and they are not goats.

Some people are like mules. Mules can be difficult to get moving. Their dedication to staying the same is bigger and heavier. They may even exhibit intentional obliviousness about the feedback being given, "I have no idea what you're talking about." A feather will not redirect a mule, neither will a bamboo rod. What is sometimes needed to get the attention and cooperation of a mule is a 2X4. With board in hand you may have to rear back, wind up and smack a mule upside the head. Your message may be blunt, to the point and insistent upon the behavior change with consequences ready should the change not happen. This is what it takes to get the cooperation of some people.

Those new group leaders who are nicer than I am cannot imagine themselves ever using a 2X4 and being so direct. This is because they assume everyone is a butterfly. And using a 2X4 on a butterfly would be cruel. Do you know what you get when you use a 2X4 on a butterfly? You get a grease spot where the butterfly once was. There are small groups that have butterfly stains on the walls and furniture, reminders of the people who used to attend but no longer do because their spirits were crushed. Do you know what you get when you use a 2X4 on a mule?–His attention. That's all usually. They just now are paying attention. "You talking to me? You want me to do what differently? Oh, OK." People who are mules, not bad, just cluelessly entrenched in a dysfunctional behavior, typically don't feel the pain we might fear. They truly are just now getting the message.

How do you know if a person is a butterfly, a goat or a mule? Start with a feather. If it works, he was a butterfly. If it doesn't work, try a bamboo rod. If it works, he was a goat. If it doesn't, use a 2X4. If it works, he was a mule. If it doesn't, he may be a wolf. There are people, who are of a predatory nature, who go to groups looking for people to prey upon. People who are only looking for what the group can do for them, without regard for the cost to the group, without regard for the mutuality of care given, are wolves.

They may be looking for people to exploit and then move on. People who refuse to be mutually committed to guidelines designed to protect the group may be wolves. The best thing that can be done with a wolf is to quarantine them. Get them out of the group. Because of the potential consequences should you get that determination wrong, you will definitely want the input of your coach or pastor before taking a step as severe as dismissal from a group.

So don't redirect butterflies with 2X4's, you'll make a mess. Don't tickle mules with feathers, it's a waste of time. Don't be negligent in your responsibility to redirect, it's what helps a group to feel safe.

Here's What Successful Facilitation Looks Like:

- Group leader prepares probing questions to open up discussion that are appropriate to the stage of group development.

- Group leader does active listening 2/3rds of the time by reflecting content and feeling, at the level shared, with a tentative opening.

- Group leader offers feedback when needed; Validating common human experiences, using Active Wondering to challenge current thinking, giving Constructive Critique that is behaviorally specific and Genuine Compliments that are character related and behaviorally specific in appropriate timing so as not to minimize the person's experience

- Group leaders redirect breaches of group guidelines respectfully and confidently, explaining what behavior won't be done in group and what behavior can be done in group.

- Group leader redirects persistent guideline violations outside of group time. The leader clearly, firmly and respectfully describes what behavior won't be done in group and what behavior can be done. The leader is clear about the need for compliance with the guidelines as a contingency for ongoing involvement in the group.

Chapter 8:

CLOSURE–FOR A SINGLE GROUP SESSION AND FOR A MULTI-WEEK GROUP SERIES

CLOSURE IS SOMETHING most people inherently avoid. I think it is because of the fear of facing loss. We've all suffered loss and none of us are too keen to experience more. Closure is intentionally embracing the end of a chapter or an experience, and acknowledging the loss of certain good things that have been enjoyed in that season. Rather than do that, most people would prefer to just walk away, to simply stop coming a week or two before the last meeting. Most people would prefer to just move on and unconsciously cease participating in this experience that's about to be over.

That's a shame because so much is missed when there is no adequate closure. This is true — especially when it comes to small group life. Without closure we miss the celebration of all the lessons learned, the wisdom and strength gained. Without the celebration, these things can be glossed over, minimized, dismissed even, as being of little to no consequence. Without closure, there can be no planned next step that takes into account the recent growth trajectory and momentum. Instead, we randomly wander off into the next thing that comes down the pike. It's a pity because with just a little effort and a strategy, we can gather up all the good that's been accomplished, reinforce it and thoughtfully direct people to their next best growth opportunity. So let's consider the strategy for ending a group meeting and then the end of the group itself.

Here are some things to consider as you prepare to end a group meeting:

- End the group on time.
- Use summary statements that reflect themes and patterns for the group time.
- Bring closure for the individuals.
- Prayer.
- Crisis intervention if needed

End the group on time. Closure takes a committed decision to do so and a little time to pull it off. Without both of these your group is likely to end past the designated ending time. If you are regularly late ending your groups, some people may interpret this to mean that you don't respect their time. Some people have time restraints, their babysitter needs to be home at a certain time or they haven't seen their family all day and if they don't get home by a certain time the children will be in bed. Or some people may be introverts at the very end of their extroversion capacity.

In any case you have a contract of sorts. You have advertised that you will provide a group on a certain topic that starts at a certain hour and is finished by a certain hour. On these conditions, people have agreed to give their precious time to attend your group. You want to honor people by honoring your word and end your group on time. If people decide to linger and visit, that is their choice. But if someone has a reason to leave precisely at the close of group, they can go without feeling as though they missed out on group work or were in some way not as loyal as those members who were able to stay later.

If you are to end group on time, you can't wait until time to quit to begin thinking about ending. Small groups are somewhat like trains. They take some time to get up to speed and they take some time to get stopped because of their momentum. If the group has reached a measure of depth in their self-disclosing, they will need a little time to put deep things back in their safe places and come back to the surface where it is safe to live everyday life. It's kind of like a deep sea diver, who if he ascends too quickly feels a pain known as the bends. Some things can't be rushed. Putting deep feelings and memories back in their storage place takes a little time.

Because the group can be lost in the thoughts and feelings of the group discussion, they may need a little warning that the end is coming. This allows them to prepare. It will be your job to keep track of the time as well as the process. Keeping an eye on a clock and setting a stop time in your mind some minutes ahead of schedule will allow you to bring the group to a close on time. Ten minutes may be enough for some groups. You may find that your group needs a little more time. If so, then adjust the end time in your mind accordingly.

I find it helpful to sit across from a wall clock if there is one in the room. This way I can discreetly keep track of the time without repeatedly looking at my wrist watch and giving the impression that I can't wait for group to be over.

Use summary statements that reflect themes and patterns for the group time. Offering summary statements is a skill that helps the group decompress from deep emotional work. Summary statements are a way of capturing the accomplishments the group has made and reinforcing them in the minds of the members. In the course of the evening a lot has been said. Part of that was some thinking out loud; attempts to get at the gems of insight that the Holy Spirit revealed. Some of the discussion has been a process of working ideas like a carpenter works wood into the shapes that are useful. When you do summary statements you are lifting up the finished product from the midst of the sawdust for all to behold and appreciate.

Giving the group a sense of what they have accomplished in a particular meeting time gives them a sense that it's OK to stop here. Something significant has been done and our time was worthwhile. Reviewing the themes discussed in this meeting directs the group members' minds away from further work and brings them back around for one last concise declaration of the lessons learned just now.

Summary statements should be a short statement of the main insights from the group discussion. It is critical that you be as concise as you are able. If you regress into an attempt to reteach all the points of the lesson, you can actually obscure the learnings. You are offering some triggers to recall to the group members' memories the main points they have discussed. You are presenting an outline of the chapter they and God have just written. This helps them to reinforce the lessons in their minds.

To be able to offer summary statements at the close of group, I try to keep track throughout the group time of themes and patterns in the discussion. I'm thinking about how what the last person has shared relates to what the previous people have shared. Usually there is a common thread because group discussion is a little like group free association. What one person says sparks ideas in the minds of those listening of similar things in their life and experience. Sometimes I can pick up the themes as I go adding what each one has said to the previous ones. Sometimes I find it easier to just let a couple of people share and then look at their thoughts and feelings collectively. No matter how I do it, I have to remind myself throughout group to make a few mental notes.

Some beginning leaders may want to take written notes to help them keep track of what's been said. This can be done if some things are taken into consideration. A person who shares his deepest darkest secrets and watches someone else taking notes might understandably get a little paranoid. People will be wondering if you are writing about them, what you are writing about them and what are you going to do with it? If you are going to take notes, I'd ask permission from the group first. I'd explain that it is to help you capture the group's learnings for review at the end and that you will destroy the notes in front of the group each evening. If even one person expresses any hesitation, I'd quickly offer to cancel my plans for note taking. Even if you do start out taking notes, you want to get to the point where you can do summaries without notes.

At the beginning of learning to lead groups it can feel like you are trying to remember an awful lot. That's because you are. But it does get easier with practice. Creating summary statements makes more sense and it becomes easier to see the patterns and remember them as you gain experience.

Closure for the individuals. Inside the issue of bringing closure to the group process there is also the matter of bringing closure to each group member's process. In some ways, we do open heart/open spirit surgery in any of our small groups where people share vulnerably of themselves. It would be irresponsible for any surgeon to allow their patient to leave the hospital without closing up the incision. People wouldn't last very long on the streets with a gaping hole in their chest. You want to make sure that you don't send anyone home with gaping emotional holes either. The first key aspect to bringing the group's evening to closure is to remember to save time to do so.

We've talked about bringing general closure to a group using summary statements and reflecting the themes and patterns of the evening. This works well when the discussion has been at an intellectual level or a moderate emotional depth. Sometimes you may notice that one or more of the people in the group have touched something deeper. You might notice that someone is tearful, quiet, looking at the floor or expressing some other non-verbal or even verbal message that suggests they've hit something deep. We want to help that person feel safe and put back together enough to leave our group and go back to his everyday life.

Leaving yourself some time at the end of the group comes in very helpful in a situation like this. It will take a moment to bring some closure. If you give the impression that you are rushing him to get himself back together so you can end group on time, you may push him into a premature, incomplete closure. This could leave him vulnerable outside of the safe atmosphere of group.

One way to begin to address an open heart may be so obvious that we miss it. Don't be afraid of the direct approach:

> *"I notice that you are tearful. It seems that we've touched upon something for you. Can you tell us a little about what's happening for you now?"*

Your direct acknowledgement of his emotional reaction invites the person to clear his mind and heart. Saying what he is experiencing and having it heard and acknowledged can bring a sufficient measure of closure. Usually this emotional expression is evidence of future work that needs to be done, but just speaking it can bring enough closure that the person can wait until the next opportunity to safely work on the issue. Be sure to reflect the feeling and content of what the person shares so they know they have been heard. Remember too, you are inviting him to share. The group member may decline the invitation with, "I'm fine." In which case you trust his judgment about what he needs for closure and honor his decision to say no more at this time.

This is a good time to offer genuine compliments in the nature we have described previously. This may seem like a contradiction of our principle from our chapter on giving feedback; to not be too quick with compliments that could minimize the pain the person is experiencing. What allows us to do this now and not seem dismissive, is that this compliment comes at the end of an evening full of active listening (I hope). Through active listening a context of caring has been established by the overall tone of the group. This also comes when the group recognizes it is time to bring things to a close. The group has the expectation that the conversation can't go on forever and bringing things to a close is not a sign of indifference but of timely necessity. A positive affirmation here can have the effect of offering hope and validation for both the person and for God's process, which is under way.

An example of a compliment we might offer at a time like this could be:

"It is apparent that you are open to the work God is doing in you this evening. We trust that God is faithful to pick up where we leave off at the next available opportunity."

Or

"It takes a lot of courage to let yourself feel these feelings and receive these insights and trust that God will bring to completion the good work he's begun in you."

Prayer. As the final cap on the evening I like to end in prayer. I find that people are receptive to God's involvement especially if they are feeling vulnerable. In these prayers I ask God for protection for the work that has been done and for the hearts that have become tender through our time together. I frequently ask God to put his seal on all that has been accomplished in our time so that no good thing that we've received would be lost. I also invite His watching over us individually until we meet again.

This is not a time to sneak in a sermonette you've been dying to deliver that will straighten out the group. This isn't waving God's magic wand over people's problems to resolve them. Prayer is not intended to be the silver bullet that fixes everything. Even though prayer may bring comfort, the intention is not necessarily to make people feel all better.

There are two powerful outcomes to this kind of praying. One is that it invites God to come do these things and I believe He will. Secondly, this kind of praying sets faith filled expectations in the hearts of the group members. This type of prayer gives a mental picture to the people that God is taking care of them. When group members can see the vision of God holding their lives together, they can more easily rest in confidence that this is true for them. Group members may still have feelings of discomfort and unrest, especially if they are in the middle of what will be an extended season of life transformation. But prayer like this may help ground people and connect them with God's power in a way that enables them to press on into the lessons at hand.

Crisis Intervention

You could go many years leading discipleship groups and never experience what I'm about to address. Even if you plan on leading support or recovery groups, the odds that you'll encounter this are small. But because the odds are not zero, I'd rather take a minute to talk about how you handle an emotional crisis.

If someone has touched something so painful that they are feeling hopeless and depressed, these normal closure skills alone may not be enough. If you have any suspicion that a person may be so discouraged they cannot see a way to go on, if you have any thought they could be feeling suicidal, then we must take more immediate action. Typically, the thought of encountering something this intense can cause a group leader to have a panic attack. Certainly this is one of those times that is a matter of life and death. Having a plan can help reduce your own anxiety.

Invite the distressed person to stay after group for a minute to chat with you. When you can get him away from the group for some privacy, you can assess for suicidal thoughts. This may seem very frightening and intimidating. It does for most veteran group leaders too. But with a few simple questions and a bit of courage, we can help. You may feel it comforting to you to have another group leader, coach or prayer team member with you.

Leading a group with a co-leader builds in a partner right from the start. If you are leading a group at the church that is part of a bigger event, like Recovery Night, Men's or

Women's Community, reach out and invite a coach or pastor to join you in caring for your group member. If you explain the inclusion of other leadership as gathering the best team we can to assist the person, most people in distress will not have a problem with inviting a new person into the conversation. I explain this by saying, "I've invited this person in to help us take care of you. I'm concerned you are really hurting. I want to make sure we've done all we can do to support you." Most people, if they are really hurting, will tolerate the involvement of a new person who at least carries the credibility of being another leader in the church.

Some beginning group leaders have the fear, "If I raise the issue of suicide and the person wasn't suicidal, I might give them ideas." In my experience this is not the case. There is enough taboo about suicide that if a person isn't having thoughts of suicide they will emphatically say "no". The greater danger is that if a person is suicidal and no one has the courage to talk about it with him, if left alone with the thoughts and feelings, that person is in more danger of acting on them.

Here is a progression of questions that will help you determine how vulnerable the person is. With each "yes" answer (for the first 5 questions) the risk is higher.

1. In light of the pain you're in, has the thought come to you that it would be better to not be alive?
2. Has the thought come to you that you could end your life?
3. When the thought comes, does it come with a picture of how you could end your life?

4. What is that picture?
5. Do you have the means available to you?
6. Who do you know who can be with you now? (The high risk answer is a too small support network.)
7. Who or what keeps you from acting on these thoughts? (Having some future orientation is good, having no future orientation is dangerous.)
8. What do you think we need to do to keep you safe from these thoughts? (You determine if you feel confident the plan is sufficient.)

If the person's first "no" response comes by at least question 3, I would consider this a lower risk situation, especially if they have a future orientation and a possible support network of friends and/or family they are willing to involve. Here are things you can do in a low risk situation to help a person stay safe.

Lower Risk

- Making sure that they won't be alone.
- Making a verbal contract: "Can you agree with me that if the thoughts to end your life come so strongly you're not sure you can resist them, you will talk to me, the Pastor on call, or the emergency help line (Research what that number is in your area) before you take any action on the thoughts?"

If the person's first "no" response doesn't come by the time you're asking question 5, I would consider them to be at moderate risk. Better with support, worse with none. Here are things you can do in a moderate risk situation to help a person stay safe.

Moderate Risk

- Separating them from their means of suicide, get drugs, gun, car keys away from them.
- Making sure they won't be alone.
- Making a written contract.
- Making a plan for getting professional help, with an accountability measure.

If a person gives "yes" answers to questions 1-5 and has no future orientation or support network, we would consider that they are at high risk. Even if the person answers all the questions right, if I have doubts, through intuition or divine guidance, I err on the side of caution. Here are things you can do in a high risk situation to help a person stay safe.

High Risk

- Separating them from their means of suicide, get drugs, gun, car keys away from them.
- Making sure they won't be alone.
- Make a plan for getting to a hospital, use family, friends, 911.

Remember to err on the side of caution. Also, group leaders should always inform their coach and supervising Pastor of any possible suicide situations. There is safety in consultation and collaboration, for the person at risk and for the church.

Here's what successful closure of a group meeting looks like:

- Group leader initiates wrap up 10 minutes prior to advertised ending time.
- Group leader summarizes main themes discussed.
- Group leader acknowledges and reflects any last significant emotion expressed within the group. If anyone is distraught, group leader invites him to stay after group and individually assesses his emotional and physical safety.
- Group leader ends with prayer inviting God's closure to the work of the evening.

Bringing closure to a group series

I want to offer a brief idea about bringing closure to a group series. This occurs more frequently when doing a support or recovery group that's doing a book or DVD study. The group is planned to last as many weeks as it takes to get through the chapters of the book/DVD. It also happens when a congregation is doing an all-church study with small group meetings that match with the weekend teaching and end when the series is completed. But even with an ongoing discipleship or life group there comes a time when an ending is indicated.

First, I give members a chance to express their feelings about the group ending. Some people may express sadness. This may have been their first time opening up to people authentically and vulnerably and being treated with love and respect. If it is the first time, they may fear that it could be the last and only time they'll get the chance to have such a wonderful experience. It's important for those feelings to get expressed and for the group to hear them. When you the leader, practice active listening and are a calm, peaceful presence, it helps the group to hear the meaningful impact they've had on one another without feeling guilty because it is ending.

Next, I pose a question to the group something like this, "Remember back (however many weeks or years) when our group began. Remember the person you were then, what you thought, what you felt and what you were doing. Now, compare that person with the person you are today. What's different?" Then I listen as people recount the growth they've experienced. When someone shares something, I reflect it back of course, but I also ask, "What else?" Often times I get a surprised look that says, "Isn't that enough?" I smile and quietly wait as though to say, "No, I bet not." It's not uncommon for the person to come up with another thing. "What else?" I continue to "What else" them until they cry uncle and say, "That's all I can think of."

The reason I push is because the natural tendency of human beings is to remember the worst about ourselves and minimize the good. I want to press each person to give a full, thorough and accurate accounting of all that God accomplished in them during our time together. As a person shares, other group members can give confirmation that the inventory of good things is true. If it has been a group of long duration, I might even ask group members to call out growth they've seen in each other. It can be incredibly affirming and encouraging to hear genuine acknowledgment from people you've lived life with for a season.

I do this for two reasons. One is that seeing and confessing the positive growth in ourselves is a skill. As a skill, one can be good at it or bad. Most of us are not so great at it. The thing about skills is that with practice, ability increases. I want the people in my groups to get good at recognizing and giving thanks to God for the good work he has done in them. The second reason is that calling out all that has been accomplished confirms our time together has been profitable so it's OK that it be done now. We have something for our investment of time and effort.

What's next?

Then, with clear memory of all that's been accomplished, I lead the group in discussion about what's next. Spiritual growth is a process not an event. I want the people in my groups to retain and build upon the progress they've just realized. The best way to do that is to keep moving forward. When it comes to spiritual growth, standing still usually results in going backwards. So I urge the group members forward. It will help if you research what other growth opportunities are available in your church or area churches to give people options to consider. People are more likely to make a decision to engage in ongoing growth when called to do so. And that's how lives are transformed, a little at a time, in a relational context that's authentic and safe. We create the time and space for people to gather and connect with God and he does his amazing work. There really is no more exciting miracle than the miracle of a changed life. And now you know how to facilitate that encounter for people.

Chapter 9:

CONTENT VS. PROCESS

To DIG DEEPER into what makes for a powerful group, let's consider the difference between teaching content and facilitating a learning process. In fact, I want you to imagine a continuum. To the far left of the continuum is 100% teaching content. At the far right is 100% facilitating process. The middle is, therefore, the varying degrees of teaching content and facilitating process in combination, 80/20, 70/30, 50/50 etc.

Teaching content   Facilitating Process

|_____|_____|
100%   50/50   100%

Both content issues and process issues are unfolding simultaneously anytime we lead people in learning. The nature of the learning experience will determine to what degree each will play a part. Acquiring and retaining new information can be accomplished with the transmission of content. Learning what application is appropriate and how to carry out the application requires a process. With this picture in mind we should probably take a step back and give clear definition for what we mean by content and process.

Content is what we will study, and process is how we will learn. At the far "content" end of the continuum are classes that we teach. In a class, for the teacher there is an emphasis on information transferal. There are facts the teacher possesses and wants the students to hear, retain and leave with. So, she focuses on organizing the information in a way that makes sense and is more easily remembered. The teacher develops an outline and decides what information to present in what order. She may make decisions about what information must be edited out because of time or the need to not overwhelm the students. A lot of thought goes into shaping the "what", or the content, of what we want to teach.

In a class, students focus on content comprehension and mastery. When they have satisfactorily grasped the concepts with no remaining questions, then the content work has been completed.

And so, a teacher decides how much time is given to conveying content, and then considers the process. She will think about what audio/visual or media support to use. She will think about activities that engage the student. Perhaps there will be some class discussion or an in-class project that teams will work on and then present to the whole class. She does this because she understands that people learn in different ways. Some learn visually, some from what they hear; others are kinetic learners and must do something, like note taking, to lock in new information. Most people learn better if they are engaged in ways that combine all of these learning prefer-ences. We pay attention to making the students active and not passively sitting there because we know that how we engage the students determines what they will retain. But between the two, in a class there is more emphasis on teaching content than on the process.

A discipleship group may decide to do a Bible study or book study together. This could be very much like a class. However, because of the backdrop of ongoing relationship and doing life together, there is a shift toward more time in process which necessitates a little less time on the content. A support group that is doing a book study would also devote some time to delivering new content to the students. But the group spends a significant amount of time discussing how the content is impacting the members.

It has been demonstrated over and over again that insight alone does not guarantee growth or change. There is still more work to do, process work. At the same time the person is working to gain understanding of the facts, he is reflecting on his current state in relation to the material. It may be that he is becoming aware of deficits, errant beliefs, shortcomings or growth edges. He may be grappling internally with whether he is ready to take ownership of his present beliefs, feelings and behaviors as the content brings them to the surface.

People wrestle with applying new learning and with what changes they must embrace if this new learning is true. They may be weighing the cost of the growth presented to them and deciding if they're willing to pay that cost. Some people would rather cling to something they know deep down is wrong, but is familiar and comfortable, rather than endure the pain of embracing something new, that requires growing and changing.

And some people are just ambivalent in the moment about making up their mind. They need a little time to thoroughly test the new thought to make sure it is worth the effort of growth and change. They might play devil's advocate with an idea as a way of trying it on for size. This doesn't mean that they won't eventually get around to embracing the lesson. It's just their way of thinking this belief through and not just blindly accepting someone else's word.

The facilitator supports students' work by asking probing and clarifying questions to encourage self-exploration. The facilitator uses active listening, reflecting thoughts and feelings and validates common human experience. The facilitator urges group members forward to apply new content to their specific life circumstances.

We do a group that is at the far "process" end of the continuum. It is our catch-all group. If you have an issue that we don't have a specific group for; such as stress management for left-handed dyslexics with food allergies and the fear of heights, then we send you to this group. Because people are coming with a variety of presenting problems, it is nearly impossible to come up with a book or video that would be relevant to everyone's situation. So this group is heavy on process. The leader sets out the group guidelines and gives a general statement of purpose for the group. Group members have the opportunity to talk things out. They find commonality in how their various experiences have affected them;

whether they've felt betrayed, disappointed, depressed or angry. Group members get feedback if they want it and we make sure that no one has to go through their stuff alone. The leader opens up the discussion with some general questions:

---

1. *If this is your first time to share in group, what brought you here?*

2. *If you've been with us and have shared before, what's different about your adversity, especially anything that's better?*

3. *If you're a veteran of the group and have shared 4 or more times previously, then, what's different about you since you've been working on your adversity?*

And then the group is off, discussing whatever is on their hearts that evening. The bulk of the time is spent sharing, listening, reflecting, asking for and receiving feedback, expressing emotions, evaluating behaviors and wrestling with decisions to make changes. Sparingly, throughout the discussion and usually towards the end of the meeting time during the closing summary, the leader may slip in a mini-teaching pulled from his own personal files of lessons learned. These are usually concise and to the point of the evening's discussion. In this group, process dominates content.

This is why we encourage small group leaders to use active listening skills two thirds of the time and require that support/recovery group leaders do so. We can tell who is doing the most work by who is doing the most talking. The group members can't do their work if the leader is doing all of the talking. If we have a leader who can't stop talking, we reassign them to a teaching role. Both teaching and group facilitation are valid roles but they are different roles accomplishing different objectives. Teaching helps students gain needed knowledge they don't already possess. Facilitating group process helps people make applications of truth into their lives. We don't let leaders dominate the group conversation and think they're facilitating group process.

Understanding Content vs. Process is important for facilitating an individual's learning experience. We pay attention to what the students will learn and how they will best learn it. Content vs. Process also has relevance when guiding the small group as a living entity. Content describes the work we are here to do; Bible study, book study, accountability group, support or recovery group, life sharing. Process describes how we will do this work as a group.

Darryl came to me concerned about an interaction that happened in his group. At their last meeting, the group was doing a Bible study. At first, things seemed to be going well; people appeared to enjoy taking turns reading passages of Scripture and the discussion questions seemed to be getting people comfortable with sharing. "At one point however," Darryl explained, "one of the members, Rob, started taking an adversarial tone."

Rob began saying things like, "How could God really intend for us to take this passage literally?!" and "I don't think it's realistic to expect that in our day and culture people could actually follow this verse." The verses he was objecting to were not particularly controversial and were part of the church's agreed upon theology. So Darryl was taken back by the stance Rob was taking and the defiant, resistant tone he was using.

This was especially troubling to Darryl because Rob's response was contrasted sharply by Karen's reaction to the study. Throughout the discussion Karen was asking questions but her questioning was different. "So what do you think God is trying to say here?" she'd ask, or "So what this means is this ...., right?" Karen's questions seemed to express an openness to learn while Rob's did not.

Darryl was concerned that he had done something wrong. How was it that his group leading could prompt learning and growing in Karen and provoke resistance and rebellion in Rob?

I proposed to Darryl that perhaps he had done nothing wrong and that his group leading was being equally successful for Rob as it was for Karen. At this point I had Darryl's attention. He was curious to know how there was anything good in what Rob was saying and how he might not be the failure as a group leader that he felt he was.

I explained to Darryl that at any given time there are two dynamics at work, content issues and process issues. This is true for the individual as well as for the group. Content issues are the "what" issues, process issues are the "how" issues. Content speaks to "what work will we do?" And Process speaks to "how will we get that work done?"

As I said before, content issues for a group might be, "What are we here to do in general?" Are we here to do a

Bible study, a book study, discipleship, support / recovery, outreach, intercessory prayer? What will we be doing or dis-cussing this evening in particular? Will we do worship, have a prayer time, have a teaching, have a discussion? These ques-tions get at what we're going to do. While this is going on, the group is working on another level.

The content work is more evident because it is on the surface, plain to see. The process happens at an underlying level, and is not so apparent. Process issues take the form of unspoken thoughts such as:

- So who's in charge here anyhow?
- How come the leader is in charge and I'm not?
- Can I be in charge?
- If I'm not in charge, will there be a place for me; what's my role?
- Where do all these other people fit in?
- Will the group receive what I have to offer?
- Does the group have anything to offer me?
- Is this going to be worthwhile?
- What's acceptable behavior and what's not acceptable?

These questions get at how we will operate together to get work done.

Perhaps you are acquainted with the stages a group goes through: Form, Storm, Norm, Perform, Reform. People Form a group when they first gather together. They Storm as they test the group and the leader to know what can be expected. They agree upon the Norms for the group; what the proto-cols, guidelines and normal ways of behaving together will be. At last the group can finally Perform the work that was the reason for gathering in the first place. When the group has completed its reason to be, the group ends, and closure is brought. People decide what their next step in growing will be and so Reform according to the nature and structure of the next experience. Process work is what enables the group to navigate through these stages successfully.

Content and Process working together looks like the story we just heard. Karen was working on content issues. She was asking for clarification. She was reciting the new learning as a way of rehearsing it in her mind and getting it established. This is good because information has to be understood to be used, but that's just the beginning of growing.

Rob was working on process issues. His words suggest that a deeper struggle was going on. We don't yet know what that struggle is, but it sounds like Rob is arguing internally and perhaps with God about some impending change in his beliefs, his behavior or in his life. And he may get a little closer to making that change because of this opportunity to wrestle and fight.

The passion of Rob's arguing says less about his likelihood to accept the learning than it does about the intensity of the issue the learning is pressing on. When a new learning challenges long held beliefs or touches on pain from the past, a person can have a strong negative reaction and still work through the emotion to get to the growth step. Having someone who knows how to facilitate that process can increase the chances he will get there. That's where the group leader comes in.

Facilitating content work is probably the more enjoyable work for beginning group leaders and the easier of the two because people are more receptive to it. It can be done by presenting new information that challenges thinking and by answering questions. It can also be done by reflecting back the content of the stories the group members share. It is amazing how helpful people say it is, to have what they just said paraphrased back to them. Capturing the who, what, when and where of the member's story allows him and the rest of the group to examine the wisdom that God may be surfacing in the group discussion.

Facilitating process work can be more challenging and less enjoyable at first because people may be more emotional in general and cantankerous in particular. But to the veteran group leader it can be the most rewarding part of the job, because this is the point at which real change and growth is about to occur.

The key to facilitating the process is to focus in on the emotion. When people are telling their stories, if they mention an emotion, be sure to include that emotion in your reflective statement. It gets more challenging when people don't speak of an emotion but only display one. In Rob's case Darryl can facilitate Rob's process by offering the following reflective statement:

> *"It sounds like you are struggling with what this verse seems to be saying and feeling a little perturbed that God would ask this of us?"*

This response acknowledges the place at which Rob finds himself in his struggle. It helps Rob get in touch with the thoughts and feelings that are stirring within him. He will Then be able to decide what he's ultimately going to do about them. Reflecting the emotion with no judgement attached demonstrates that the group is a safe place to be honest about having struggles, to Rob and to all the other group members observing the interaction. Other group members may be holding a private struggle within themselves as well. And it gives a heart to heart connection to Rob, which gives him strength to get through his struggle.

Here's what this supportive, reflecting statement does not necessarily do. It doesn't immediately resolve the issue for Rob. There is no magic that automatically turns Rob from a questioning dissenter into an agreeable and compliant student. Which leads to the other skill a group leader must practice here to facilitate the process… self-restraint.

After offering this very supportive statement, the most likely response the group leader will get is a little more grousing and resistance, perhaps with a little more passion this time. And what the group leader can do at this point is let the objections hang in the air. Allowing a little silence lets the weight of the words fall on the shoulders of the one uttering them. The silence communicates that there is no anxiety on the leader's part that this member isn't getting on board and toeing the company line. It promotes a sense of peace and safety within the group. Perhaps the only thing left to say is:

---

*"Thanks for your honesty about where you are Rob.
Who else has something to say about this verse?"*

To attempt to rush in at this point and convince Rob that he must accept the consensus understanding is likely to elicit greater resolve on his part to differentiate from the group and stand alone in his opinion. Once the case has been made for a particular idea the next best thing to do is to leave it alone. For the group leader to back off now puts the full responsibility for what Rob will choose to believe and what he will choose to do with his life on Rob's shoulders.

But how can a group leader do this? How can a leader not push in when a member is obviously disregarding the plain truth? Only by trusting the process and with regular practice does a leader get comfortable allowing time and space for the Holy Spirit to work in someone's life. God has created a whole world of autonomous beings with free will and He is overseeing the whole creation. It can be a scary thing to let a person leave your group with only the Holy Spirit following after them to lead them into all truth (John 16:13), but it can be done.

Many people will come to our groups with toxic beliefs that they picked up at other churches before coming to ours. We can see that God will have to help us undo some things in them so that he can build some better things in their lives. But if we don't encourage people to think for themselves and trust God's Spirit to convict them of sin and of righteousness (John 16:8), then we are likely to continue the cycle of saddling them with some errant doctrine of ours that the next church will have to fix.

Unless you are absolutely confident that you have completely, fully and accurately, without flaw, divined the mysteries of the infinite God, then It's best that you learn to trust the process and learn to facilitate the process along with the content.

At the core of the matter for the group leader is this: Who is responsible for being in charge of this person's life? It is easy for caring people to be drawn into the notion that they are somehow responsible for the people in their group. (Some people feel responsible for every person in the world. Whew!) We have to come to grips that ultimately God and that person are responsible for his life, what he will believe, what he will feel, what he will do. We are not responsible for the people in our group. We are responsible to them for how we interact with them, to treat them with dignity and respect. We are responsible to give them our best, but we're not responsible for what they choose to do with our gift. Having clear relational and problem ownership boundaries is critical when facilitating groups. So, let's consider the topic of boundaries a bit.

Chapter 10

BOUNDARIES IN MINISTRY

IT IS CRUCIALLY important to stick with the strategy of walking along side of a person and not taking charge of her life by deciding for her what she ought to do. The temptation to analyze, give advice or fix people grows stronger in the face of a steady barrage of painful issues. When presented with the intensity of what gets talked about in a support group, some beginning group leaders panic and fall back into these old habits. Being courageous and standing strong in facilitation skills instead of "fixing" skills is what makes support groups work to bring the healing of God and to empower people to live more effectively. It also helps discipleship groups to facilitate greater growth and life transformation. After empathic listening, the ability to have healthy, appropriate boundaries is probably the next most critical element to doing safe, effective small groups and having longevity in ministry.

It's easy to see the problems associated with the extremes of boundaries, too few and too many. Too few boundaries result in chaos in which productivity and effectiveness are lost. Too many boundaries produce a rigidity in which love and care are lost.

I want to offer two confessions in regards to boundaries. There was a time in my life when I had no boundaries. I was driven by obligation and the pressure to please people and to always meet their expectations. As a minister I felt like it was my job to represent God well to people. I knew that God had no limits and that led me to work as though I had no limits. But the reality was that I did have limits. I had limits of time, energy, money and mental health. That last one threatened to run out the fastest. When I didn't acknowledge my limits and I exceeded them, I began to feel burned out, exhausted, resentful, bitter and hopeless. It became clear that I wouldn't last long in ministry at that pace.

So I took a class where I learned about the skills of Warmth, Empathy and Respect. In the respect teaching I learned about problem ownership and not taking other people's monkeys off their backs and onto my own. Monkeys were our metaphor for the problems we all face. I learned that the most respectful thing I could do for people was to be honest about my limitations and to not build up resentment and bitterness towards them for imposing so much upon me (even though I said yes) and then blast them for it at a later date.

I was learning about boundaries and how to say the word "no". This was life saving for me. I was so excited about my new deliverance from the stress of over extending myself that I used "No" with great zeal. I was making up for all the time of not being able to say no. I was quick and confident in my saying "no". This was liberating and life giving to me, but I came across as being closed off and uninterested in helping other people.

I recognized there are actually two questions people are asking when they ask for what sounds like inappropriate rescuing that exceeds healthy boundaries.

1. "Will you care-take me and do what I'm responsible to do?"
2. "Will you care about me and the predicament I'm in?"

If I'm not careful, when I answer "no" to the first question, they can hear "no" to the second question. My answer now is:

"I bet we can come up with something that will help your situation. I don't know if I can do exactly what you're asking, but I'm pretty sure we can come up with something that will help."

I start by answering the second question with an affirmative response. "Yes, I am interested in you and your predicament."

This answer reframes the issue from whether I will take on responsibility for their problems, to my willingness to join them in a partnership in which they are still primarily responsible to live their own lives and solve their problems. After affirming my willingness to join them, I clarify my limit, I say "no" in a gentle way, "I'm not sure I can do exactly what you're asking me to do." For some people, this will be enough and they will be open to new ideas with my help. For some, they might persist in trying to get me to take responsibility for their lives and their problems. As they persist, I get more pointed in saying "no".

From:

"I'm not sure I can do exactly what you're asking me to do."

To:

"I don't think I can do that part for you."

To:

"No, I'm not going to do that..."

I'll get into more detail in a minute about how specifically I set and enforce boundaries. But I want to share my second confession about boundaries with you. My first is that I started out with no boundaries when I first began to do ministry. Then, after I learned about boundaries and I was in the counseling field, I had this belief that strong boundaries were the epitome of good mental, emotional health. I would judge how healthy a person was by the strength of his boundaries. If he had clear boundaries that he held to, he was healthy; if he did too much for people, I determined he was less healthy.

I was in a small group of mostly mental health professionals and we were studying the book Hiding from Love, by Cloud & Townsend. One of my friends, who was a counselor, came to the group one night with a proposition that I found very disturbing. From reading the book, he was starting to question this notion that boundaries were the defining standard of health. He pointed out that by the strictest application of problem ownership guidelines, Jesus violated those guidelines when He paid for our sins. Problem ownership says, "My sin, my problem. I am responsible to solve the problem. Jesus could support me but I need to solve the problem." But

Jesus determined that I could not solve the problem of my own sin, so He took it upon Himself and He felt the weight of my sin on the cross and died in my punishment so I wouldn't have to.

My friend went on to assert that co-dependent behavior would look a lot like sacrificial love on the outside. The difference would be on the inside, with the motivations, where it's really hard for another person to judge. From the book, my friend concluded that love would endure injustice after injustice for the hope of redemption. Love would suffer abuse after abuse, apparently unto death, for the hope of seeing someone turn from evil.

16And so we know and rely on the love God has for us. God is love. Whoever lives in love lives in God, and God in him. 17In this way, love is made complete among us so that we will have confidence on the day of judgment, because in this world we are like him. 18There is no fear in love. But perfect love drives out fear, because fear has to do with punishment. The one who fears is not made perfect in love. (1John 4:16-18 – NIV)

If I fear being taken advantage of, if I fear being abused, I am not yet perfect or complete in love. As a group we reasoned that if we do not have enough love in our hearts to suffer abuse upon abuse without getting bitter and losing sight of that person's redemption, and we may in fact, not have enough love in our hearts for that, then we should use boundaries for our protection. And on that evening we all agreed that we did not. Boundaries are God's protection for us while we are in progress. In light of not yet being made perfect or complete, boundaries are God's concession and gift to us.

And the reality is, that there are many times that I do not yet have enough love in my heart to endure abuse after abuse for the sake of redemption without the threat of losing my inner peace. So it is right for me to have boundaries. But this is a far cry from boundaries being the ultimate measure of emotional health. Boundaries are God's concession to me while I get healthier and stronger.

I did not like hearing this!!! It completely messed with my perfect little model that protected me from ever being taken advantage of. This idea threatened to steal from me my plausible excuse for never having to be inconvenienced again while doing ministry. Fears of falling back into my previous co-dependent behavior came rushing back. But I couldn't defeat the logic of what my friend was suggesting to us.

That's been some years ago now. I've had some time to wrestle with this issue of boundaries. I have come to some agreement with the thought that strong boundaries are not the ultimate measure of health, but come second to true sacrificial love given freely without false guilt or misguided obligation.

I think that boundaries do protect me while I am still growing in love, still being healed by God's love. The truth is that I may never reach the level of healing and strength that permits me to endure the kind of suffering for others that Jesus did. And I think that there is a rule of problem ownership that is wise for us to follow. God can override that guideline whenever He wants because He has perfect judgment. I think we will do well to ask ourselves if the help we are about to offer will empower the person to grow stronger or enable the person to stay stuck, sick and weak. I think the butterfly has to fight its own fight to get out of the cocoon or it will die. The baby chick has to fight its own fight to get out of the egg shell or it will lack the strength necessary to survive in the world.

And I think that God allows the problems that come to us to come for a purpose. I believe that God allows trials that will challenge us and cause us to grow strong. I believe that God permits problems that take us to the end of ourselves and our sinful, self-reliant, godless coping mechanisms so we will at last fall on our knees before Him, putting our trust and dependence on Him. I believe that if we rescue people from the pain of problems God has orchestrated or at least commandeered, we steal away their motivation for yielding to God and interfere with His working.

I believe there is a place for sacrificial service to others and a place for boundaries in ministry. So let me share some guidelines that help me in deciding upon and using boundaries in ministry.

Guideline 1

Have good reasons for the boundaries you set. The reasons should have benefit for the people you're trying to help as well as you, not just for you. People are fed up with bureaucracy. That happens when boundaries and limitations only benefit those who are supposed to be the servants of the public good. We don't want to perpetuate that kind of frustration.

But a boundary of fifteen people maximum for a small group might be good for protecting the experience of the group attendee. With more than that, shy people may not feel comfortable sharing personal things. Perhaps not everyone will get to share as much as they need. If the group leaders are new, they may not be able to keep the group focused and on target with so many people. So that's a boundary that provides benefit to the members.

One of the support groups at our church asked if they could have the boundary that we don't take people who walk in our group after we've gone through the guidelines. They felt like it reduced the sense of safety when they saw late-comers not abide by the guidelines by giving advice or not maintaining a self-focus. So we added that as one of our guidelines.

Having the boundary that our prayer teams don't meet people off site for additional prayer protects the pray-ers from accusation that they did something inappropriate if the pray-ee gets mad or hurt at what is said or done. But it also protects the pray-ee from inadvertently drawing the prayer-or into a counseling role that she may not have the training for and the expertise to do. It also keeps the pray-ee from attaching dependence upon the pray-or that really belongs on God.

I could see that in a ministry to the poor, having bound-aries about how much a person or family can take at one visit, would help ensure that those people who come later will still find resources available. Limits also protect people from developing an unhealthy dependence upon the ministry that might prevent them from eventually growing strong enough to take care of themselves and their family.

Guideline 2

Know your own boundaries and those of your team. You may have more liberal boundaries than those of the min-istry you serve with but it is important to honor your team's boundaries. If the team is not unified in what boundaries are set and how they are held, it creates confusion for the people you serve and chaos for the people you serve with.

First of all, after reading 1 John 4:16-18 about perfect love casting out fear, it may feel like a failure to admit that you are not yet made perfect in love and therefore need boundaries. I remember first reading that scripture and thinking, "Oh my! This is the standard I'm supposed to be at, having no fear? I better start pretending that I'm there right now!"

I feel confident that the reason God inspired that verse to be written was not to produce shame, denial or pretending. I don't think this verse is saying, "You should have no fear and you should be perfected in love!" I think the purpose of that verse is simply to give us a reality check and a wake-up call that being captured by God's love is very much a process. And if you still have fear, then you haven't arrived yet, so don't rest on your laurels. Keep opening yourself up to God's love. Do you know how many people still have fear and are not yet made perfect in love? Almost all of us!

Almost all of us have some worry about something in the future. If we were completely captured by God's love, we would have no worry. Almost all of us fear some catastrophe, either in the world or within ourselves. If we were made perfect in love, our confidence in God would be so great we would have no fear. But we do, most of us. So we keep pressing on. And I keep using boundaries as necessary while I'm pressing on.

With practice I have learned how to accurately assess where I need boundaries. The clue to discerning between sacrificial love in action or something codependent is what's going on inside of my heart, especially in terms of motivations.

It takes some real self-honesty to distinguish between true compassion and the desire to avoid the unpleasant feelings of someone's anger because I wouldn't do what he wanted. It requires courage to recognize my inclination to avoid the pain inherent in walking along-side of someone going through a difficult trial. The best clues are in my self-talk. If I hear things like, "I gotta...", "I should...", "what they will think about God depends on me...", or "I just hate to see them hurt so I'll just..." then my motivations may be coming from something more self-driven than others- driven. I don't want to act on those impulses. If I have a true sense that God is prompting me to do something sacrificial, then as a rule, I try to obey God.

One check and balance for confirming God's leading is when the question of boundaries comes up in the course of serving as a team. The scriptures say:

1Everyone must submit himself to the governing authorities, for there is no authority except that which God has established. The authorities that exist have been established by God. 2Consequently, he who rebels against the authority is rebelling against what God has instituted, and those who do so will bring judgment on themselves. (Romans 13:1, 2 – NIV)

Paul writes these words about the secular rulers like kings and governors. So if it's true that we should follow leaders who don't know God, it makes even more sense that we should follow ministry team leaders who do know God and have set certain boundaries for our team to follow.

If your personal leanings are contrary to the protocols and procedures your team has set, this is not a time to follow your gut without checking with your leaders. If after you plead your case for why you think this is an exception, if they approve it, you're good to go. If your leaders decide to stick with the boundaries in place, you'd do well to follow the leadership God's placed over you. If you feel very strongly otherwise, pray for your leaders and your team to change their minds. But don't act apart from their authority.

Besides the issue of obedience to God through obedience to our leaders, there is the practical element of the chaos that is introduced into a system when some members of a team are providing care one way and others another way. People who are wrestling with God about taking the discipleship step he's calling them to will run from the team member who's holding them accountable and run to the one known for being a soft touch. So know your personal boundaries and those of your team.

Guideline 3

Explain the boundary in terms of benefit to the person and/or the larger group as a whole. The reasons may be disputable. Just own them as your reasons or the ministry's reasons.

Remember the work you did in guideline one to only choose boundaries that have a good reason? When holding a boundary with someone, explain the good reason especially the part about how it benefits him and the others in the group. Adults like to understand things. When you have to say "No" to someone about something, explain why. Then they feel more like an adult. When you issue edicts and dictates without explanation, insisting on blind compliance, you treat people like children and they are likely to take offense to that.

So say, "This is our guideline and this is why we have it…" Don't spend a lot of time defending it. That implies that you feel insecure and uncertain about it and that it might not be a very good guideline but you're trying hard to convince them. Just explain it in as calm a tone of voice as you can, with as much clarity as you can, with as few words as possible. If you sound confident, most people will buy in. Those that don't buy in because they want what they want, will still figure out that you're serious about your boundary. You can validate their displeasure for any inconvenience or difficulty, but don't apologize for the boundary. It's there for their good and the greater good of everyone else.

Guideline 4

When telling someone "No" to something, tell them what you can say "Yes" to. This helps me as the guideline enforcer to feel like less of a bad guy. But more importantly, it gives people a sense of empowerment. People take redirection down a different road better than they do running into a brick wall. It also lets people know where the boundaries are so they can self-direct their behavior with confidence in the future. This helps when doing a redirection as we talked about in chapter 7.

- No, you can't give advice, yes you can share your experience.
- No, you can't monopolize the conversation, yes you can have a turn.
- No, you can't focus on people not in the group, yes you can talk about you.
- No, you can't have a side conversation while someone else is already talking, yes you can speak next.

This strategy helps to keep group members from shutting down and going silent. This strategy can also help you the leader feel more confident that you're not being mean, you're simply giving direction that protects the group experience.

Chapter 11

THOUGHTS TO KEEP IN MIND

A LOT HAS BEEN covered in this book. If you're thinking about leading a group for the first time, don't be overwhelmed by what you've read here. Certainly one reading of a book can't give you mastery of group facilitation skills. These things take time and experience to learn. Relax and have grace for yourself while you are learning. In the introduction I described how we follow the class with an apprenticeship. That's where most of the learning actually takes place.

Look for a mentor. It will feel safer to begin co-leading with someone who has been facilitating groups for a while. The mentor can be responsible for the wellbeing of the group. You, the apprentice, can then be responsible to just learn something each meeting. Ideally that mentor would be from your own church and supervised within the leadership structure of your church, i.e. a coach or pastor. However, if your church doesn't yet have small groups, consider reaching out to a nearby church that does. At our church we welcome students from other churches to attend our training. Hopefully you can find one close by who will do the same for you.

If none are available, consider attending various open 12-step groups in your community. Look for those that seem to be well run. Watch to see if the leader is using the skills you've read in this book. If they are doing the skills well, they can be a model for you to follow. While I prefer to learn from someone who shares my faith perspective, it isn't essential in this case of looking for an example of the facilitation skills being done competently. One of my mentors once told me, "All truth is God's truth, no matter who claims to have discovered it or is teaching it." Obviously you want to be more selective when seeking a mentor for matters of faith and spiritual practice.

Also, don't start by leading the most difficult groups. Beginning group leaders will do well starting with small groups where people share life together and encourage one another in their spiritual development. As you get more skilled and more confident you can tackle bigger challenges like a discipleship or an accountability group. Eventually, if you desire to, you could facilitate a support or recovery group. But even among those there are degrees of difficulty. Leading a boundaries group is easier than leading a sexual abuse recovery group. Lean on your church leaders to help you grow in your proficiency.

If you've led groups for a while and realize that you didn't know to do much of what we cover here, don't begin doubting the validity of your previous work. God uses us at whatever level of development we are and He is the most significant element for leading successful small groups. Even after you have mastered everything covered in this book you will recognize that at any given group meeting, God is doing the heavy lifting.

I do think that putting in the effort to learn these skills is worthwhile. God's power changes lives. These skills create a conduit for God's power to flow through our relationships with one another. The better our relational skills are, the larger the pipe is for God's love and power to pour through. The group leading you did before was valuable. God's love and power came through the pipe you had at the time. Should you decide to apply yourself to learn these skills, I believe you will see your influence increase as the pipe diameter increases.

I also want to speak a bit about the measurement of success. It is tempting to gauge your success by how much people grow and heal while under your care. It certainly is gratifying to watch God set people free or watch people grow in their faith and commitment to God. That used to be what I looked for to measure my effectiveness.

But here's the problem. There were times when I knew I hadn't done well at faithfully executing my strategy. I got hooked by someone's story and fell into fixing instead of listening. I gave self-disclosures that took the focus off my group and put it on me. And sometimes, even when I was off my game, amazing things happened. People confessed shortcomings. People repented of their sins. I saw forgiveness offered and received. There were other times when I was on. My listening was accurate and to the heart. My boundaries were flawless. My probing questions insightful. And, the people seemed unimpressed and the energy in the room fell flat. I often left a group meeting exhausted and discouraged. I knew I had worked hard. I just wasn't sure it made a difference.

At some point, probably a low one, I was questioning what I was really trying to accomplish through our support/recovery groups. A new thought entered my mind. If someone became less dysfunctional, less co-dependent, less depressed, less anxious, less angry and left our groups not knowing Jesus and how much he thought of them, our work would be fruitless. I concluded that entering into a Christ-less eternity with good boundaries would be little consolation.

If on the other hand, if despite our best efforts, the depressed person was still depressed, the addicted person was still addicted and the codependent person still felt responsible for the world BUT they each knew and trusted Jesus, then the essential and necessary part that absolutely must happen, happened. In trusting Jesus, they gave themselves more chances to grow and heal eventually. If it didn't happen on this earth, it would eventually happen when they were clothed with immortality. Whatever work was yet incomplete at the time of their leaving this world, Jesus would be faithful to finish the good work that was started here.

I knew I couldn't be responsible for whether people embraced Jesus, but I could be accountable for whether people had a chance to encounter him and know him in our groups. Did we bring the Kingdom of God with us? That is, did things happen in our groups like they happen in God's Kingdom? If people experienced truth and grace, we succeeded. If people were treated with kindness and respect, we succeeded. If the distressed were comforted and the comfortable were distressed by God's challenges, then we succeeded. If people felt safe enough to be real before God and man we succeeded.

I am persuaded that if people lay down all their pretense and masks in the presence of God and his truth they will be changed. So my new personal mission is this, to make the church the safest place on earth to be authentic before God so more churches can see the miracle of a transformed life.

I have heard stories of people being hurt in church. Sometimes it's because we have high expectations around church life that aren't realistic and so disappointment is assured. Sometimes the people themselves bear some responsibility in a conflict and don't see it. So to their telling they are victims of abuse of authority. But there are times when well-meaning church people do or say things with the greatest intentions of faithfully carrying out what God asks of men. Yet they are mistaken and misguided. And so there are people who have stories of receiving harsh treatment at the hands of God's representatives. Their experiences are often their excuses for giving up on church if not on God altogether.

So my hope is to see the church become less likely to wound someone and more likely to facilitate wholeness. I want churches and group leaders everywhere to know how to create the space for people to encounter the Spirit of Jesus and then know how to stay out of his way so he can do his work in their hearts. I pray that will be your experience in your group leading days ahead. May God bless you to do exactly that, Amen!

To get free teaching and study resources for
Unleashing the Power of Small Groups, go to
www.markalutz.com

To learn more about what people in your small group
might need and what you can do to be of help,
check out this other Mill City Press book by Mark Lutz
What is Wrong With People?!

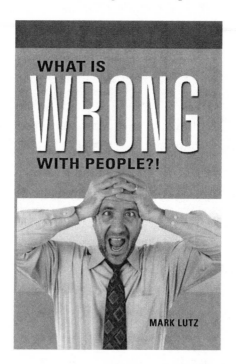

CPSIA information can be obtained
at www.ICGtesting.com
Printed in the USA
FFOW03n1924290817

9 781545 603406